White Christmas

The Story of
an American Song

Jody Rosen

Scribner

New York   London   Toronto   Sydney   Singapore

SCRIBNER
1230 Avenue of the Americas
New York, NY 10020

SCRIBNER and design are trademarks of Macmillan Library Reference USA, Inc.,
used under license by Simon & Schuster, the publisher of this work.

For information regarding special discounts for bulk purchases,
please contact Simon & Schuster Special Sales at 1-800-456-6798 or
business@simonandschuster.com

Designed by Kyoko Watanabe

Set in Baskerville

Manufactured in the United States of America

1 3 5 7 9 10 8 6 4 2

Library of Congress Cataloging-in-Publication Data
Rosen, Jody.
White Christmas : the story of an American song / Jody Rosen.
p. cm.
Includes index.
1. Berlin, Irving, 1888– Holiday Inn. White Christmas. 2. Popular music—
United States—History and criticism. I. Title.

ML410.B499 R67 2002
782.42'1723—dc21   2002030877

ISBN 0-7432-1875-2

Permissions acknowledgments appear on page 214

To my parents

Contents

I'm dreaming of a white Christmas
Just like the ones I used to know,
Where the treetops glisten
And children listen
To hear sleigh bells in the snow.
I'm dreaming of a white Christmas
With ev'ry Christmas card I write:
"May your days be merry and bright
And may all your Christmases be white."

1

Introduction: The Hit of Hits

✦

Fingers on the black keys: Berlin at the piano, mid-1930s.
Rex Hardy Jr./Time Inc., Courtesy of The Irving Berlin Music Company.

published number, written when Irving Berlin was still Izzy Baline, a nineteen-year-old singing waiter in a Chinatown saloon; in 1984, "My Wife's Gone to the Country (Hurrah! Hurrah!)," his first hit; in 1986, "Alexander's Ragtime Band," his career-making smash, whose clarion opening line—"Come on and hear"—announced not just the arrival of a national troubadour but a young country's liberation from Victorianism and swaggering emergence into the century it would claim as its own.

The old man may have grieved the loss of his songs to the public domain, but much of his catalog had made that journey years before, migrating from Tin Pan Alley straight into national lore. He was born in Siberia, yet seemed to have a direct channel to the American imagination, yanking song after song out of the collective unconscious and returning them to his adopted country as beguiling reflections of its hopes, myths, and passing fancies. He strove to write, he said, "in the simplest way . . . as simple as writing a telegram." In so doing, he filled the American Songbook with pop standards that sound as inevitable as folk songs; his songs are definitively twentieth-century things—"a Berlin ballad" appears in Cole Porter's "You're the Top" alongside a Waldorf salad and Mickey Mouse—yet they strike us as timeless, anonymous. We recognize George Gershwin's musical signature in the bluesy grandeur of "Summertime" and "The Man I Love"; the droll, debonair voice of "Too Darn Hot" and "Miss Otis Regrets" is unmistakably Porter's own. But in Berlin's most celebrated songs—"Alexander's Ragtime Band," "A Pretty Girl Is Like a Melody," "Always," "Blue Skies," "Puttin' On the Ritz," "How

Deep Is the Ocean?" "Easter Parade," "Cheek to Cheek," "Let's Face the Music and Dance," "God Bless America," "There's No Business Like Show Business"—Berlin is invisible. It was not an insult when Alec Wilder, in his landmark study of American popular song, declared himself at a loss to describe stylistic common denominators in the songwriter's vast output.

Berlin's most famous song, by far the most valuable copyright in his (or anyone else's) catalog, is "White Christmas." But as I discovered in writing this book, it may be the Berlin hit least associated with him. Everyone I spoke to about "White Christmas" knew the song; everyone had Bing Crosby's dulcet, definitive recording lodged in his mind's ear. Yet few knew who composed it. This wasn't true just of my contemporaries, who like me had grown up with hip-hop and rock 'n' roll and whose only exposure to Irving Berlin may have been Taco's synth-pop travesty of "Puttin' On the Ritz." I met avowed Berlin fans who not only were unaware that the man had written the tune, but could hardly comprehend that it had been *written* at all. They assumed "White Christmas" was as old as the hills, its creator as ancient and unknown as the composer of "God Rest Ye Merry Gentlemen."

But "White Christmas" is a pop song: you could call it *the* pop song. Berlin liked to brag that the number "was a publishing business in itself," a rare instance of the songwriter—no slouch at trumpeting his successes—selling himself short. "White Christmas" is the biggest pop tune of all time, the top-selling and most frequently recorded song: the hit of hits. It is a quintessentially American song that the world has embraced;

among the untold hundreds of "White Christmas" recordings are versions in Dutch, Hungarian, Japanese, Swahili, and, in a knowing nod to its creator's pedigree, Yiddish. Sales of "White Christmas" records have topped 125 million copies.

Bing Crosby's original version on Decca Records remains a music industry landmark. For over fifty years it stood as the best-selling record in history. Introduced in the 1942 film *Holiday Inn* (it won the Academy Award for Best Song), Crosby's "White Christmas" held first place on the Hit Parade countdown for a record ten consecutive weeks; it would reenter the survey every December for the next twenty years (excepting 1953), spending thirty-eight weeks in the top spot and an unprecedented eighty-six weeks on the chart. All told, Crosby's "White Christmas" has sold over 31 million copies; it was unseated from its place in the *Guinness Book of World Records* as the all-time top single only by Elton John's Princess Diana tribute, "Candle in the Wind '97." (Crosby's record reentered the British charts for two weeks the next year—forty-five years after its initial release.)

Popular culture is infatuated with novelty, and pop music is particularly unsentimental, ruthlessly turning today's superstar into tomorrow's one-hit wonder, forever seeking refreshment in new styles, new sounds, the next big thing. Once a year, though, the Christmas season brings songs from several centuries back to jostle for airtime with the latest hits. "White Christmas" is a newcomer to the Christmas canon— the composer of "Joy to the World!" beat Berlin to the punch by at least two hundred years—but in the decades since its appearance, it has become the most performed of all seasonal

songs: the world's favorite Christmas carol. To this day, it continues to generate tens of thousands of annual record and
sheet music sales. The Muzak versions that fill the nation's
malls each December should alone be enough to pile-drive
"White Christmas" into the consciousness of unnumbered
future generations of shoppers.

Although Crosby's remains the signature version, singers
won't leave "White Christmas" alone: every year brings new
versions by performers that run the musical gamut, from the
Mormon Tabernacle Choir to the German heavy metal band
Helloween. The list of "White Christmas" performers includes
many of the most famous names in twentieth-century popular
music: Bing Crosby, Louis Armstrong, Frank Sinatra, Ella
Fitzgerald, Nat King Cole, Charlie Parker, Fats Domino, Elvis
Presley, Aretha Franklin, the Beach Boys, Smokey Robinson
and the Miracles, the Supremes, the Temptations, the Four
Tops, the Jackson Five, Willie Nelson, Bob Dylan, Barbra
Streisand, Bob Marley and the Wailers, Al Green, U2. Berlin's
melody has been reimagined as a stuttering punk anthem; as
Wagnerian Sturm und Drang with a chorus of thousands wailing in the background; as a loping country ballad; as a string
of quicksilver bop improvisations; as a thudding house track—
a carol for an Ibiza Christmas. Otis Redding wrung new
pathos from the old song, recasting it as a Memphis soul ballad; Michael Bolton did a laughable Otis Redding imitation
and recorded what may be the most overwrought "White
Christmas" of them all (and consider the competition). Is
there another song that Kenny G, Peggy Lee, Mantovani,
Odetta, Loretta Lynn, the Flaming Lips, the Edwin Hawkins

Singers, and the Backstreet Boys have in common? What other tune links Destiny's Child, The Three Tenors, and Alvin and the Chipmunks; Perry Como, Garth Brooks, and Stiff Little Fingers; the Reverend James Cleveland, Doris Day, and Kiss?

But the song's power transcends its sales figures and commercial ubiquity. With "White Christmas," Berlin created an anthem that spoke eloquently to its historical moment, offering a comforting Christmastime vision to a nation frightened and bewildered by the Second World War. But it also resonated with some of the deepest strains in American culture: yearning for an idealized New England past, belief in the ecumenical magic of the "merry and bright" Christmas season, pining for the sanctuaries of home and hearth. Its dreamy scenery belongs to the same tradition as Currier and Ives's landscapes and Robert Frost's "Stopping by Woods on a Snowy Evening." The song's images of sleigh rides and falling snow and eager children capture the mythic essence of the American Christmas. "White Christmas" seems to have always existed, lurking, as one Berlin biographer has written, "just beneath the surface of national consciousness." Indeed, in writing "White Christmas," Berlin lit on a universal ideal: the longing for Christmas snowfall, now keenly felt everywhere from New Hampshire to New Guinea, seems to have originated with Berlin's song. It can safely be said that London bookmakers didn't offer odds on the possibility of a white Christmas prior to "White Christmas."

From the beginning, the song has been a blank slate on which Americans have projected their varied views on race, religion, national identity, and other heady matters. In Philip

Roth's *Operation Shylock,* "White Christmas" is an emblem of "Jewish genius," in Kurt Vonnegut's *Mother Night,* a wearisome reminder of the Second World War. In the early 1940s, at the height of its popularity, "White Christmas" was a huge hit among both white and black audiences. In the decades since, African-Americans have viewed Berlin's anthem with increasing ambivalence, detecting in Crosby's placid "white-bread" crooning a coded message excluding blacks from the national Christmas celebration. The song became a hit in the winter of 1942, when it was embraced by homesick American GIs as a symbol of the country to which they longed to return and the values they were fighting to defend. It was the war's unlikely anthem: a "Why We Fight" song in which the fight was never mentioned. Some thirty years later "White Christmas" returned to play a role in a more troubled American war: the U.S. military used it as the secret signal instructing American soldiers to evacuate Saigon.

One of the most poignant "White Christmas" battles was waged by Berlin himself, when the songwriter launched a fierce (and fruitless) campaign to ban Elvis Presley's recording of the tune. Today, Berlin's rage at the rock 'n' roll "desecration" of his song looks like nothing less than a lament over the sunset of an entire pop culture era: the period, roughly bounded by the two World Wars, that the songwriter had stood astride and whose passing plunged him into a depression that dogged the final forty years of his life.

We remember that interwar era as the Golden Age of American Song—the charmed period when Berlin, Jerome Kern, the Gershwins, Rodgers and Hart, Porter, Harold Arlen, and other titans of Broadway and Hollywood turned the pop song, once regarded as the crudest kind of mass entertainment, into a definitive national art form. In the twenty-first century, the song standards remain indelible; consecrated in the recordings of Sinatra and Fitzgerald and Armstrong and Billie Holiday, launching pads for the improvisations of successive generations of jazz greats—they are the bedrock of American pop. Their lush melodies and lyrical bon mots conjure a fairy-tale world of urbanity and romance, generating nostalgia even in those of us born decades after their heyday. They are supreme products of what historian Ann Douglas has called America's postcolonial phase; listening to song standards—from "Tea for Two" to "I Get a Kick Out of You" to "Over the Rainbow"—we hear the optimism of the American empire at its giddy early height.

I grew up in a very different musical age, with ears conditioned by the urgency of rock and soul and hip-hop, and the song standards always struck me as exotic. In part, this book was inspired by my curiosity about the music—where it came from, why it blazed and disappeared. Historians hallow song standards as one of the United States' great gifts to world culture; musicologists parse their structure with the same loving scrutiny they lavish on Schubert lieder. Yet the American Songbook remains misunderstood, distorted by the culture war that erupted when rock 'n' roll remade American entertainment in the 1960s. In one corner is the they-don't-write-'em-like-that-anymore crowd, who have mystified the song-standard era beyond reason and recognition. For those of us who love "Cheek to Cheek" and "Star Dust" and "Papa's

Got a Brand New Bag" and "Don't Believe the Hype" in equal measure, it can be galling to read history as told by champions of classic pop, who cling to the notion that all craft and charm drained from American music the day rock and soul's barbarians stormed the gates. On the opposite side are rock critics who, steeped in rock's rebel mythologies and cult of authenticity, have effectively read fifty years of pop—and George M. Cohan, Irving Berlin, Al Jolson, and Bing Crosby—out of musical history.

These competing mythologies remove the song standards from their historical context, and the story of "White Christmas"—the era's commercial zenith, the signature collaboration of its most famous songwriter and singer—brings that context into sharper focus. It was a time before rock 'n' roll introduced a musical generation gap and put the voices of blacks and Southern whites at the forefront, before Vietnam and the social ruptures of the 1960s, when pop songs seemed to embody cultural consensus—when the American middle class sought charm and reassurance in mass entertainment. Today, our longing for that musical era grades into a larger nostalgia for the mystical heyday of the "Greatest Generation," that allegedly happier period of stalwart American values and national unity. If any song represents mid-century consensus, it is "White Christmas": a celebration of the de facto national holiday, introduced by a multimedia father figure in the midst of a World War, when circumstances encouraged an unprecedented uniformity of thought and feeling. Song-standard aficionados might argue that music was simply better in the good old days. But one can't help suspecting that they are also longing for a simpler time, when pop songs spoke almost exclusively in the voice of the white middle class and hadn't yet begun to reflect the difficult questions and moral ambiguities of American life.

Nevertheless, if the songs of that pre–civil rights, prefeminist period strike us today as blithely ethnocentric, it should be remembered that they were the result of a social struggle in many ways as significant as those that have inflected rock's history. The pop-song industry was dominated in both its creative and commercial spheres by Jews—many of them, like Berlin, recent immigrants—and the music it gave to the world was the music of assimilation, a distinctly New World concoction: the result of a people's striving for social acceptance and a piece of the American pie. Much of twentieth-century pop culture is a kind of Yankee Doodle Yiddishkeit: All-Americanism as imagined by Lower East Siders, intoxicated by showbiz and its fast track out of the ghetto. "White Christmas"—a Russian-born cantor's son's ode to a Christian American holiday—is a milestone of Jewish acculturation matched perhaps only by another Berlin magnum opus, "God Bless America": a symbol of the extraordinary way that the Jews who wrote pop songs, sang them on vaudeville stages, invented Broadway, and founded movie studios, turned themselves into Americans—and remade American pop culture in their own image.

Familiarity has made "White Christmas" remote: we know the song so well that we barely know it all. Bing Crosby begins singing, and we hum along, or flee the room; in any case, our ears are closed. But listen again: "White Christmas" is an oddity, whose melody meanders chromatically and is filled with unexpected moments, somber near-dissonances. Strangest of all is the song's underlying sadness, its wistful ache for the bygone, which—in contrast to chirpy seasonal standards like "Jingle Bells" and "Santa Claus Is Comin' to Town"—marks "White Christmas" as the darkest, bluest tune ever to masquerade as a Christmas carol.

"White Christmas" isn't my favorite song; it isn't even my favorite Irving Berlin song. I prefer "Blue Skies," with its shades of exultation and melancholy, or the brooding "Let's Face the Music and Dance." Down the years, those songs have kept their streamlined gleam; with its mile-wide sentimental streak, "White Christmas" has come back in recording after recording as kitsch.

Berlin, of course, never shied from sentimentality—or anything else that pleased his audience. He journeyed far from his roots on old Tin Pan Alley, the nickname given in 1900 to the clangorous songwriters' row along West Twenty-eighth Street in Manhattan; but where his younger songwriting colleagues styled themselves as *artistes,* Berlin clung to the Alley's populist values: the public was the best judge of a song's worth, a tunesmith was only as good as his latest hit. It was an ethos that sprang from a need for audience acceptance—a trace, perhaps, of Berlin's roots as Bowery song busker—and above all, from a sense of duty. Berlin was a *public* songwriter, who pledged allegiance not to his muse but to "the mob." "A good song embodies the feelings of the mob," he said. "A songwriter is not much more than a mirror which reflects those feelings."

This philosophy made Berlin the people's choice and carved a special place for his songs in our national life. (The post—September 11 reemergence of "God Bless America" is just the most recent example of Berlin's uncanny staying power.) But to his detractors, Berlin's crowd-pleasing unmasked him as a cornball and a hack; despite the illustriousness of his songbook, he has never been as beloved by tastemakers as some of his harder-edged colleagues.

"White Christmas" is the ultimate Berlin tearjerker, and if there are more decorous songs, there are few deeper ones. We cringe at its mawkishness, but our embarrassment should arise from the shock of self-recognition: three-hankie schmaltz is, to a large degree, the American way of song. Berlin's paean to long-gone white Christmases "just like the ones I used to know" distills a whole tradition: the hopeless lust for yesteryear that runs through a couple of centuries of popular song, from the homesick ballads of Stephen Foster to Victorian parlor-room plaints to the desolate nostalgia of the blues. "White Christmas" is about as good a summary as we have of the contradictions that make pop music fascinating: it is beautiful and grotesque, tacky and transcendent. Revisiting the song's story, listening for the thousandth time to its maudlin, immemorial strains, we are reminded of a trick in which Berlin and Crosby both specialized: how, time and again, they proved that art and schlock could be one and the same.

2

The Best Song Anybody Ever Wrote

Berlin with the tools of his trade, 1942.
The piano in the background is a Berlin "Buick,"
equipped with key-changing hand-clutch.
Courtesy of The Irving Berlin Music Company.

A simple melody will always linger—
I mean the kind you pick out with one finger.
                              —IRVING BERLIN,
                "An Old-Fashioned Tune Is Always New"

W HITE CHRISTMAS" enters the written record on January 8, 1940, in the form of forty-eight measures of musical notation, jotted on a sheet of Irving Berlin Music Company manuscript paper, in the distinctive hand of Helmy Kresa, Berlin's longtime musical secretary. This earliest transcription of the song finds Berlin still wavering about its verse; nine bars in, a rather stolid melodic passage has been crossed out and improved. But tellingly, the sixty-seven familiar notes of the song's chorus are intact. Nearly three years before Bing Crosby introduced "White Christmas" to the world, Berlin brought this most famous and indelible of his melodies to Kresa as a fully formed creation.

Berlin has had many hagiographers. Perhaps the greatest of these was the songwriter himself, whose years in the rakish atmosphere of Tin Pan Alley, Broadway, and Hollywood taught him the value of legend-building and tall tales. His varying reminiscences about the creation of "White Christmas" have a back-room-at-Lindy's feel: it is hard to imagine Berlin telling the song's "story" without a cloud of cigarette smoke above his head and a slab of pastrami on his plate. He told his friend Miles Kruger, a historian of the Hollywood musical, that the song was composed in Beverly Hills. On his 1954 promotional tour for Paramount Pictures' *White Christmas* movie, Berlin unspooled a different version of the story nearly every day. The *Los Angeles Mirror* reported that Berlin had written "White Christmas" "for a Broadway show called *Stars on My Shoulder* . . . on an August afternoon in 1938 in his Beekman Place home in New York"—a home that he hadn't in fact moved into until 1947. In an "exclusive interview" with *The American Weekly,* Berlin recalled that he had written the song in 1940, "for a revue." "When I wrote 'White Christmas' in 1941," he explained at a press junket in Philadelphia, "it was devised really to fit into a situation in the motion picture *Holiday Inn.*"

A more trustworthy recollection was that of Helmy Kresa, who joined Berlin's staff in the mid-1920s and remained the songwriter's trusted amanuensis for the better part of the next six decades. According to Kresa, Berlin strode into his publishing firm's Midtown Manhattan headquarters with the freshly composed Christmas number first thing one Monday morning, a story that agrees with the evidence: January 8, 1940, the date that Kresa noted in the top right-hand corner of that first lead sheet, was a Monday. Berlin's appearance at that hour would have startled his employees, who were unaccustomed to seeing their boss before one or two in the afternoon. His early arrival, they must have known, could mean only one thing: Berlin, who never learned musical notation, had written a new song that he was anxious to have Kresa fix on the staff.

All-night songwriting sessions were the norm for Berlin, a lifelong insomniac whose frenzied work habits were as celebrated as his songs. The newspaper stories that greeted Berlin's early fame as the hitmaking phenom of the ragtime craze called him a "songwriting machine"—a bit of a backhanded compliment, linking the young star to the crude industry of Tin Pan Alley's song mills. But there *was* something machinelike about Berlin: he was astoundingly prolific—at his productive peak he was writing a song a day—and no one who encountered him could help but be struck by the impression of a man in a state of whirring motion. ("He's a buzz saw," marveled a reporter who visited Berlin in 1942. "He's Mr. Energy.") He composed continually: jotting lyrics on shirt cuffs, on cocktail napkins, on hotel stationery, dreaming up new tunes on overnight train trips, in elevators, at poolsides, in front of the shaving mirror. He wrote "Alexander's Ragtime Band" in the middle of a clamorous vaudeville rehearsal and "Anything You Can Do" in a taxi marooned in Midtown traffic. When Queen Elizabeth congratulated Berlin on "My British Buddy," his World War II–era ode to Anglo-American camaraderie, he replied: "Thank you, ma'am. I wrote the song in a bathtub." In 1912, a month after he married for the first time, Berlin told reporters that his new bride had cured him of the "night-to-morning and morning-to-night" songwriting compulsion that had made him "a nervous wreck . . . all music, all songs, all the hope of song hits." Five months later, his wife was dead, of typhoid fever; Berlin returned for good to his insomniac

regime and became the nation's pop-song poet laureate—
America's nervous wreck. All told, Berlin wrote thousands of
songs and published 812 of them, an amazing 451 of which
became hits. An undated lyric fragment in Berlin's papers at
the Library of Congress is the cheery confession of a man who
recognized his creative drive as a kind of mania:

> *He wakes her up and cries,*
> *"I've written another song,*
> *You've got to listen to it!"*
> *She rubs her eyes and answers,*
> *"I don't want to hear it . . ."*
> *He keeps it up all morning,*
> *Until the day is dawning . . .*
> *And then he wakes her up and cries,*
> *"I've written another song!"*
> *She has to listen to it;*
> *She simply cannot keep him shut—*
> *He's a nut, he's a nut, he's a nut.*

This song-crazed "nut" is a figure Helmy Kresa would have
recognized: throughout his decades of service, he went to bed
knowing he might be roused in the wee hours by a phone call
heralding the arrival of a new tune. Kresa was hired by Berlin
in late 1926 as one of several staff arrangers. By the early
1930s he had become Berlin's main musical secretary; though
he would go on to write a hit song of his own, "That's My
Desire," and serve several other of Tin Pan Alley's most celebrated composers—Porter, Harold Arlen, Johnny Mercer—

Kresa was always known as Berlin's right-hand man and remained in his employ until shortly before the songwriter's death in 1989. Like Berlin, Kresa was an immigrant—his heavy German accent gave him an air of "longhair" musicianly gravitas—and he shared his boss's devotion to musical modesty: simple chord progressions, harmonies that were elegant but unornate. He was famously fast, capable of burnishing a rough new Berlin composition into something playable in a hour or two of speedy work.

Kresa's job wasn't easy. Berlin was a handful; although he disavowed artsy pretension and played to the hilt the earthy role of bootstrapping street kid made good, he had a temperament worthy of a La Scala diva. He was moody—exhilarated one moment, grim and foreboding the next, one minute generous and jocular, the next brooding in stony silence, the next raging about his colleagues' inadequacies, bungled business deals, perceived slights. When he locked into a songwriting groove, he was irrepressible, dragging strangers to his piano to vet his new tunes, boasting about his successes to anyone within earshot. When the songs dried up, his spirits sank; during his worst slumps, Berlin was stupefied by self-doubt, convinced that he had lost his talent and his career was over. His driving need for public affirmation made things worse: in commercially fallow periods, other composers could take refuge in the satisfactions of the creative process, but Berlin's sense of self-worth shriveled in the absence of hits. Kresa weathered his boss's mood swings with varying degrees of tolerance and exasperation; he considered quitting many times over the years and would have done so, he confessed, "if I had not so much admiration for his fantastic genius as a writer of both words and music."

How—and where—Berlin wrote the words and music he brought to Kresa that January morning is unclear. He had spent Christmas and the New Year with his family—his second wife, Ellin, and their three daughters, thirteen-year-old Mary Ellin, seven-year-old Linda, and three-year-old Elizabeth—at his recently purchased country home in Lew Beach, New York, a rambling estate in the Catskills whose pastoral ambience, perhaps not coincidentally, recalls the scene depicted in the chorus of "White Christmas." The Berlin family returned to their Manhattan town house, a five-story brownstone on East Seventy-eighth Street, just after the New Year; in all likelihood, Berlin remained in the city for the following weekend of January sixth and seventh.

Any composing that Berlin did that weekend would have taken place in his third-floor study, whose centerpiece was a curiously homely upright piano. This instrument, which Berlin coyly called his "Buick," was custom-built: rigged with a key-changing hand-clutch to accommodate the musical limitations of its owner, who, like many Tin Pan Alley old-timers, only ever learned to play "on the black keys," in the key of F-sharp. Berlin would sit at the piano for up to twelve hours at a time, chain-smoking and wrestling melodies and lyrics into shape. "The melody doesn't come to you," Berlin explained. "You sweat it out. Lots of big successes I've written only after I've become blue in the face."

Berlin's family grew used to the noises that would drift from behind that study door: flurries of notes, piano noodlings, the odd burst of high-pitched singing—the stammering sound of a song coming to life. This ruckus followed Berlin on the road. Front-desk clerks at hotels where the songwriter stayed had to contend with calls from sleep-deprived guests; Berlin learned to muffle the din by stuffing his piano with towels and bathrobes. We can only guess at the sounds that filled Berlin's study that January weekend. But by Monday morning, they had ordered themselves into a song.

Picture Irving Berlin arriving at his office at 799 Broadway on a chilly January day in 1940. He was fifty-one years old, at almost the exact midpoint of his life. At a time when songwriters were stars on par with Hollywood screen idols, his face—with those intense, dark eyes, ringed with the "overnight bags" of a thousand insomnias—was recognizable to millions. The songwriter stood just five feet six inches, but he cut a rather dashing figure: the olive skin, the slicked, jet-black hair, the smart Savile Row suits. His trademark feature, though, was his nervous energy: the darting gestures whose madcap effect reminded his daughter Mary Ellin of a speeded-up Charlie Chaplin silent film.

That morning, there was extra urgency in Berlin's step. He pushed through the front door of his office and passed his startled secretaries without a word of greeting, looking for Kresa. He found him at his desk. Kresa was accustomed to Berlin's bluster, but even he was taken aback by the audaciousness with which the songwriter announced his latest creation, a Christmas tune. "I want you to take down a song I wrote over the weekend," Berlin said, waving Kresa into his office. "Not only is it the best song *I* ever wrote, it's the best song *anybody* ever wrote."

3

Beverly Hills, L.A.

"The sun is shining, the grass is green":
Berlin takes a dip, mid-1930s.
Courtesy of The Irving Berlin Music Company.

Christmas has woven a pattern in my life.

—IRVING BERLIN

A LISTENER WHO has cued his CD player to Mel Tormé's 1992 recording of "White Christmas" may find himself puzzled by its opening bars. A piano vamps discreetly in the background; Tormé sings in the plush, vibratoless tone that earned him the nickname The Velvet Fog. But there is a strange jazziness to the tune's saunter through a series of seventh and ninth chords, and the words that Tormé sings are unfamiliar. "The sun is shining," he begins. "The grass is green." He continues:

> *The orange and palm trees sway.*
> *There's never been such a day*
> *In Beverly Hills, L.A.*
> *But it's December the twenty-fourth,*
> *And I'm longing to be up north.*

These may be the most famous "lost" sixteen measures in popular music: the little-known introductory verse of "White

Christmas." After that concluding line—"And I'm longing to be up north"—Berlin's melody makes a gingerly seven-note descent, landing on a C major chord, and suddenly, over swelling orchestral strains, Tormé is singing the world's best-known pop song: "I'm dreaming of a white Christmas . . ."

In writing the "White Christmas" verse, Berlin was hewing to the Tin Pan Alley convention of preceding thirty-two-bar choruses with sixteen measures of mood-setting introduction. On the Broadway stage, these verses served a similar function to the recitative that precedes an operatic aria; they were often performed conversationally—a casual way of establishing the tempo and dynamics of a song and easing into its refrain. Although some composers excelled in verse-writing—the Gershwin brothers and Cole Porter were specialists in the art—verses were infrequently recorded, and almost none have lodged in public memory. Millions can hum the refrains of "Star Dust" or "My Funny Valentine," but how many people know their verses?

The opening section of "White Christmas" is doubly obscure. In 1989, Berlin wrote a letter to the singer Rosemary Clooney, a star of the 1954 *White Christmas* movie, who had performed the song's verse in a recent concert. Berlin thanked Clooney for resuscitating the verse, which, he noted, "is hardly ever used." But in December of 1942, at the height of the song's initial conquest of the Hit Parade, Berlin himself had ordered the sixteen bars expunged from its sheet music. The public had fallen for Bing Crosby's hushed, chorus-only rendering of the song; now Berlin realized that the verse's jauntier musical atmosphere and images of Beverly Hills shattered the chorus's wintry spell.

That forgotten verse points to the song's inauspicious origins: "White Christmas" began its life as a curio. In June 1938, Berlin returned to New York after spending the better part of the previous five years in Hollywood working on movie musicals. It had been a triumphant half decade. In 1932, he had emerged from a commercial and creative dry patch with the Broadway smash *Face the Music;* he followed this with a string of movie hits that not only raised Hollywood's commercial bar, but whose finest moments—Fred Astaire and Ginger Rogers twirling across a moonlit veranda to the strains of "Cheek to Cheek"—took the film musical, that collision of the two quintessentially modern American lively arts, to new heights of whirligig poetry.

That March of 1938, Berlin had turned fifty. Hollywood's New York ex-pat royalty turned out to salute the songwriter's three decades in show business at a birthday party held in a detail-perfect reconstruction of the Pelham Café, the Chinatown watering hole where the teenage Izzy Baline cut his teeth as a singing waiter. For thirty years, his restless quest for new hit-making "angles"—a favorite Berlinism—and attention to the smallest shifts in public fancy had put him on the cutting edge of an ever-changing popular culture. With *Watch Your Step* (1914), he became the first popular songwriter to mount a Broadway show comprising entirely his own songs; the first time the world heard sound in a motion picture, it heard a Berlin tune: Al Jolson belting out "Blue Skies" in *The Jazz Singer.* In the 1920s, when a new songwriting vanguard— George and Ira Gershwin, Richard Rodgers and Lorenz Hart, Cole Porter—replaced Tin Pan Alley's churn-'em-out ethos

with an artier emphasis on careful craft, melodic sophistication, and the lyrical mot juste, Berlin kept creative pace with
the upstarts but stayed just as prolific. "You make all the rest
of us feel pretty darned ineffective," Jerome Kern complained
in a letter. "We're hep that none of us is heightened by your
genius for producing just the right thing at just the right
time."

But in the spring of 1938, Berlin was slumping. *Alexander's
Ragtime Band,* the big-budget Berlin musical released by Twentieth Century-Fox that May, drew almost entirely from the
songwriter's back catalog. He managed to come up with five
new numbers for its follow-up, *Carefree,* another Astaire-
Rogers picture. But the film was lackluster: when it appeared
in August, reviewers suggested—presciently, it turned out—
that the Astaire-Rogers partnership was running out of gas.

Berlin had come home to New York intent on making an
invigorating return to the Broadway stage. The project he had
in mind was a throwback to Broadway's pre-talking-pictures
era: he wanted to put on a revue, like those he had staged so
successfully in the early 1920s at the theater he co-owned, the
Music Box on West Forty-fifth Street. Berlin's notes for *The
Music Box Revue of 1938* envisioned a woolly vaudeville-style
hodgepodge of tunes, skits, and stunts: topical songs touching
on newsmakers from Hitler and Mussolini to Joseph Kennedy
to the Dionne quintuplets; a racy comedic number called
"Found a Pair of Panties"; sketches featuring acrobats, "side-
walk comedians," jugglers, and trained dogs.

By August, Berlin's plans had moved in a more baroque
direction. The show had a new title—*The Crystal Ball*—and a

novel form: it was a three-act-long "revue of to-day, tomorrow and yesterday." According to Berlin's notes for the show, the first-act curtain would rise on a "Greek chorus" arrayed behind a proscenium arch, singing a musical explanation of the revue's unusual structure:

> *It's in three acts*
> *Instead of the usual two,*
> *And in each act*
> *We're doing a separate revue:*
> *A first act, a second, and a last—*
> *The present, the future, and the past.*

The Crystal Ball was never produced. When a new Berlin show reached the Broadway stage in 1940, it was *Louisiana Purchase,* the spry political farce loosely based on the life of Huey Long. But among the unfinished songs and jotted notes for Berlin's unrealized revue are clues about the provenance of his most famous song. Especially intriguing is a list of numbers for *The Crystal Ball*'s opening act, probably typed by Berlin himself in mid-1938:

ACT ONE—"THE PRESENT." 1939.

1. Opening—Greek Chorus—crystal ball curtain
2. Short sketch with music
3. number in one
4. sketch
5. commercial advertising
6. rhythm number

7. sketch in two
8. White Christmas—finale
Start in one going into full stage

From this earliest reference to "White Christmas" we learn that the song had existed, in some form, for at least several months prior to Berlin's breathless arrival at his office on January 8, 1940. Berlin was a fanatical tinkerer whose songs often gestated for months, or even years, undergoing several revisions before taking final shape; for every song that he completed, there were dozens of false starts and half-songs, snatches of song lyrics and piles of hastily scrawled angles that he stored for future use. The songwriter had a term for his collection of scraps and works-in-progress: "the trunk." Several of his most celebrated creations—"Easter Parade" and "God Bless America" among them—were reworked trunk songs. The Christmas number that Berlin brought to Helmy Kresa that Monday in 1940 may have been completed, as the songwriter boasted, "over the weekend," but it had almost certainly been kicking around the trunk for some time before that.

Also noteworthy is the song's position in *The Crystal Ball*'s proposed running order. "White Christmas" may at this stage have been a primitive version of the song that was eventually published—it may have been nothing more than a twinkling "angle" in its creator's eye—but Berlin obviously had a high opinion of it, deeming it a worthy act-closer.

This suggests something about the song's form: the "White Christmas" that Berlin slated for his revue's first-act finale was not the homely ballad that Crosby crooned in *Holi-*

day Inn. The songwriter was a stickler for variety-show convention, and convention dictated that first acts conclude with a visually spectacular number. Berlin's note that the number would "start in one going into full stage" indicates how he envisioned "White Christmas" being staged: the song would begin with a lone player onstage singing its verse; the curtain would then shoot up, revealing an elaborate set, and a full chorus would join in for a rousing sing-along finale.

It is difficult to imagine the "White Christmas" we know today as showstopper in a revue filled with dog tricks and pratfalls. Yet the song that reached the world in 1942 as a hymn was, in its inventor's initial conception, something else entirely: wry, parodic, lighthearted—a novelty tune.

We glimpse Berlin's original vision for "White Christmas" in the six lines of its verse. Where the chorus evokes a distant yesteryear (the Christmases "I used to know"), the verse is set in the modern present: on Christmas Eve Day in Los Angeles. There is conversational breeziness in its language ("There's never been such a day . . ."). There is, moreover, a distinct social milieu being described: we are in the louche company of Beverly Hills swells, who loll away day after "perfect day" on green grass beneath swaying trees and a beating sun.

The "White Christmas" verse is a satire, Berlin's variation on a classic New York pastime: a potshot fired at Gotham's ditsy West Coast rival. (We can hear a New Yorker's voice in the misnomer "Beverly Hills, L.A."—an error Berlin shrugged off when his wife pointed it out.) The verse paints a picture of palmy paradise that is deflated by the revelation "it's December the twenty-fourth." For the song's narrator, this "perfect

day" in Beverly Hills is no fun at all: Christmas is approaching, and what is Christmas without wintry ambience?

In the song Bing Crosby sang in *Holiday Inn,* white Christmas was a vision of snow-christened perfection; in Berlin's
original conception, it was a punch line. The sight-gag staging
of the number in the songwriter's revue would doubtless have
driven the joke home. According to biographer Philip Furia,
Berlin pictured it being performed by "a group of sophisti-
cates gathered around a Hollywood pool," pining for a rustic,
snowbound Christmas with "cocktails in hand"—a preposterous tableau sure to tickle a New York audience.

Berlin apparently so fancied this novel angle—subverting
holiday solemnity for humorous effect—that he thought it
might be the basis for an entire show. He began making notes
for yet another revue, this one built around "fifteen of the
important holidays in a year, using each holiday as an item in
the revue." The show, whose working title was *Happy Holiday,*
was explicitly comedic. "In several of the items," Berlin wrote,
"the point of view will be to debunk the holiday spirit." Once
again, Berlin gave his Christmas number pride of place: it
would be, he wrote, "the summing up of the entire show."

Behind the satirical scrim of his Hollywood Christmas
song, we discern the figure of Irving Berlin, exasperated after
a half decade spent on movie lots. Like most of America's
songwriting elite, Berlin was drawn to Hollywood by the boom
market in movie musicals that followed the 1927 release of *The
Jazz Singer.* While other members of the Tin Pan Alley diaspora
had relocated outright or bought second homes in Los Angeles, Berlin never put down roots, preferring to camp out for

months at a time in suites at the Beverly Hills Hotel and the Beverly Wilshire. In 1939, Berlin finally resolved to move to L.A., leaving his New York apartment and renting a home in the Hollywood Hills, only to back out at the last minute, pitching his family into a frenzy of unpacking and house-hunting back in Manhattan. "He just couldn't bring himself to go through with moving to L.A.," his daughter Mary Ellin Barrett would recollect. "He regarded Los Angeles as fake." As Berlin himself explained to his wife: "There's no Lindy's in Los Angeles. No paper at two in the morning. No Broadway. No city."

A poignant moment in Berlin's California exile may have provided inspiration for "White Christmas." It was Christmas, 1937, and Berlin was stuck in Hollywood, working on *Alexander's Ragtime Band.* Like many graduates of a Lower East Side Orthodox home, Berlin proudly celebrated Christmas. The songwriter's family life proclaimed his American arrival with all the trappings of post-Jewish haute-bourgeoisie style: a shiksa wife, an uptown address, a Christmas tree in the living room. Though Berlin was steeped in Yiddishkeit, his relationship to institutional Judaism was negligible: here, a Passover seder, there, a stroll down Fifth Avenue to Kol Nidre service at Temple Emmanu-El.

The Berlin family Christmas pulled out the stops. It was, Mary Ellin Barrett recalls, "the single most beautiful and exciting day of the year," with a family dinner at a "gleaming candlelit Christmas table," "enormous stockings," and "so many packages, so many toys." Invariably, these celebrations were punctuated by Berlin's retelling of a favorite story from his Lower East Side childhood: how he stole away from his pious home to the apartment of his Irish neighbors the O'Haras and gazed in rapture at their Christmas tree, which, to his young eyes, "seemed to tower to Heaven." The songwriter must have been gratified by the sight of his children at the foot of their tree, which scraped the ceiling of the family's double-storied library.

But for Irving and Ellin Berlin, seasonal merriment was tempered by sorrow. Back on December 1, 1928, Ellin had given birth to a baby boy. Three and a half weeks later, the day after Christmas, an item appeared on page 3 of the *New York Times*:

BERLINS' INFANT SON DIES
OF HEART ATTACK

Irving Berlin, Jr., 24-day-old son of the composer of popular songs and of the former Ellin Mackay, died suddenly yesterday morning of a heart attack at the Berlin residence, 9 Sutton Place . . .

The Berlins refused to see reporters yesterday and information was given out through a Miss Rorke, the nurse who had attended the child. The death occurred shortly after 5 o'clock in the morning. Miss Rorke was the only person present. Mr. and Mrs. Berlin were called immediately. Three doctors, whose names were not disclosed, were summoned, but nothing could be done, according to the nurse.

Irving Berlin, Jr., was their second child, the other being Mary Ellin, 2 years old.

Mary Ellin herself only learned that she had had a brother eight years later—the very winter her father was in Hollywood working on *Alexander's Ragtime Band*—when she happened upon a newspaper clipping in a desk drawer. The article made sense of something that had troubled the young girl: every Christmas Eve her parents, with long faces and sober attire, left the house and "went somewhere." Where they went, it turned out, was Woodlawn Cemetery in the Bronx, to lay flowers at Irving Berlin Jr.'s grave. Years later, Ellin Berlin would admit to her daughter, "We both hated Christmas. We only did it for you children." Though he put up a jolly front, the tragedy of Christmas, 1928, had forever dampened Irving Berlin's holiday cheer.

Christmas, 1937, was only the second that Berlin had spent apart from his family; that Christmas Eve, he would not make the somber pilgrimage to the Bronx. Instead, he had been invited to dinner at the Beverly Hills home of his friend Joseph Schenck, the Twentieth Century-Fox Studios CEO. Schenck was Berlin's oldest friend—a buddy from his Lower East Side street-urchin days, who claimed to have bought the first sheet music copy of Berlin's 1907 debut, "Marie from Sunny Italy." Like Berlin, he was a ruthless perfectionist in his professional affairs; he shared Berlin's taste for deli food, hours of show-biz shoptalk, and high-stakes card games. When they got together, the Old Neighborhood bonhomie was palpable: Schenck called Berlin "Zolman," and the pair traded wisecracks in Yiddish. Berlin counted Schenck as one of his few dear friends. "You said one very wise and true thing to me," Berlin wrote to Schenck in 1956. " 'As we get older, our real friends become fewer.' Apart from my immediate family, I can count mine on one hand and have a couple of fingers left over. I don't have to tell you you head the list."

The movie mogul had a surprise in store for Berlin that Christmas Eve. When the songwriter arrived at Schenck's estate, he was led to its screening room. "I have this Christmas short that I'd like you to take a look at," Schenck said.

Berlin took a seat in the screening room. The lights dimmed; the projector whirred. A title appeared on the screen: "Twas the Night Before Christmas." The title dissolved, and the camera zoomed in on the snowy exterior of a grand French door hung with a holiday wreath. Cut to the interior of a large apartment: two little girls, with their backs turned to the camera, are facing a festively trimmed Christmas tree. The camera pans in, the girls reel around to face it and shout in unison, "Merry Christmas, Daddy!" These aren't actors; they are Berlin's elder daughters, Mary Ellin and Linda, wearing Hungarian dresses, their last year's Christmas presents. The youngest Berlin sibling, nineteenth-month-old Elizabeth, is there too, splayed on the floor in front of the Christmas tree, dwarfed by ribbon-topped packages.

Schenck's "Christmas short," it turned out, was made especially for Berlin, filmed five months earlier on a Fox soundstage by the Hollywood director Gregory Ratoff. Ellin Berlin had known her husband would be spending Christmas alone and had conspired to create a holiday treat: a three-minute-long cinematic Christmas card.

Might "White Christmas" have first stirred on that Christmas Eve in 1937? We can imagine a glum Berlin, waking the next morning to a balmy, sun-strafed Christmas Day. Christmas always put him in a funk; this Christmas he was three thousand miles from his loved ones. Stepping onto the terrace of his Beverly Hills Hotel suite, he would have beheld a scene surreally different from the homey yuletide aura of his family's film: gently rocking palms, the garish green of perfectly tended lawns, a swimming pool's cobalt glare. The only snowflakes in Hollywood fell on soundstages.

The memory of that California Christmas surely played some part in inspiring the song that surfaced a few months later in his various plans for a stage revue. Berlin had little idea that beneath his Christmas-in-Beverly-Hills lampoon— stirring in the homesick "longing" of the verse's last line—the Great American Christmas Carol was waiting to emerge.

In the meantime, with his struggles to mount a revue bearing no fruit, the songwriter turned his attention to other projects—a new movie, *Second Fiddle,* and *Louisiana Purchase*— casting "White Christmas" into that purgatory where so many previous Berlin creations, slaved over and tossed off, lowly and grand, had gone before it: the trunk.

4

No Strings

＋

"Top Hat, White Tie and Tails":
Berlin and his "swellegant" muse, Fred Astaire, Hollywood, 1935.
Courtesy of The Irving Berlin Music Company.

Soon
We'll be without the moon,
Humming a diff'rent tune . . .

—IRVING BERLIN,
"Let's Face the Music and Dance"

IT IS A CURIOSITY of the American Songbook that the majority of its songs were composed during the 1930s, yet scarcely any acknowledge the hardships of the Great Depression. American popular music has never been as insulated from American social reality. When E. Y. Harburg's "Brother, Can You Spare a Dime?" became a hit in 1934, it stood out as a novelty among the ballads crooned on the country's radio shows: a stark portrait of national woe surrounded by Tin Pan Alley's paper-moon artifice.

In an odd way, the pop songs of the 1930s were a social barometer: the fervor with which the public embraced musical escapism was a measure of the hard times. And indeed, twentieth-century pop rarely produced such beguiling fantasy. The new class of songwriters that emerged in the 1920s were quintessential "young moderns," who brought a self-conscious artistry and cosmopolitan outlook to what was previously regarded as a profession for scalawags, drunks, and other shady characters who hung around the Union Square rialto. Richard Rodgers drew on the romantic composers he had studied in his conservatory training; the rich, bluesy luster of George Gershwin's compositions reflected tricks he picked up on his "slumming" pilgrimages to Harlem; the lyrics of Ira Gershwin, "Yip" Harburg, and Cole Porter betrayed their bookish taste for Gilbert and Sullivan and the light verse that filled the pages of *The Smart Set*.

By the 1930s, the new songwriters were pouring out a seemingly unending stream of witty and beautiful songs whose quality even the stuffiest highbrows could not dispute. With their sumptuous melodies and lyrics that made taut, witty poetry out of everyday speech, the songs of the thirties were an American apotheosis: popular music at its most styl- ized and urbane. Earlier popular song had had its artful moments and flashes of ruffian wit, but nothing had approached the sophistication and expressiveness of a song like Gershwin's "Embraceable You" (1930), with its daring tonal shifts and rich chromaticism. Nor was there precedent for lyrical ingenuity on par with Leo Robin's "Thanks for the Memory" (1937)—a luminous pile-up of jokes and rhymes:

> *Thanks for the memory*
> *Of rainy afternoons,*
> *Swingy Harlem tunes,*
> *And motor trips and burning lips and*
>   *burning toast and prunes.*

Songwriters brought this new sophistication to songs whose focus was radically narrowed. In the first two decades of the century, Tin Pan Alley strove for Morning Edition topicality, taking account of news events, trends, inventions—the whole mad pageant of American social experience. Now, although Tin Pan Alley was still used as a generic term to describe the music industry centered on Broadway and its Hollywood satellite, song publishers had dispersed from West Twenty-eighth Street and abandoned their old-school commitment to pop-music journalism: the new, up-market American popular song was almost exclusively preoccupied with romantic love. The task of the Broadway and Hollywood tunesmith was, in the words of one wag, to say "I love you" in thirty-two bars; from "It Had to Be You" to "All of Me" to "The Way You Look Tonight" to "I've Got You Under My Skin," the American Songbook is for the most part a catalog of variations on a single sturdy theme.

The narrow focus of the new songs was, in part, an emblem of their aesthetic modernity, their art-for-art's-sake emphasis on style above all. What mattered wasn't so much what the songs said—usually some variation on "Blah, blah, blah, blah love . . . Tra la la la, tra la la la cottage for two," as Ira Gershwin put it in his 1931 parody—but how they said it: the shape of a melody, the flair of a well-wrought rhyme or deft turn of phrase. With their thirty-two-bar form and "blah, blah love" content rigidly standardized, Tin Pan Alley's songs became sleek exercises in sheer style; this was Deco Pop, music for an era whose cult of the streamlined and pristine was expressed in everything from the cut of waistcoats to the facades of skyscrapers.

For a nation mired in the bleak realities of the Depression, the escapist appeal of these songs was considerable. Tin Pan Alley enshrined bourgeois love as a blissful sanctuary from history itself; listening to "Love Is Here to Stay" or "The Song Is You" or "Isn't This a Lovely Day (to Be Caught in the Rain)?" it was possible to believe—for the three minutes that the song played, at least—that real-world hardships didn't matter, for in romance there was a charmed parallel universe: a "world" of two. "Millions of people go by," Al Dubin wrote in one of the decade's signature songs. "But they all disappear from view . . . I only have eyes for you."

Some songs provided a more decadent escape. In the luxuriant melodies and arch, knowing words of hits like "Just One of Those Things" and "I Can't Get Started," Americans heard the voice of an alluring character: the bon vivant who sauntered through 1930s popular culture, cocktail shaker in hand, untroubled by the Depression. These "swellegant" songs were most closely associated with younger writers—Rodgers and Hart, the Gershwins, and especially, Cole Porter—who filled their compositions with drolleries and highbrow references; but it was Berlin's *Top Hat* collaboration with Astaire and Rogers that gave the fantasy its most intoxicating form. For the millions of Americans who made *Top Hat* (1935) the biggest movie musical success to date, the film's primary delight wasn't its predictable boy-meets-girl high jinks, but the swank apartments, the evening clothes, Fred Astaire catching the night flight to Venice for a weekend spree—its immersion in, as Berlin wrote in "Top Hat, White Tie and Tails," "an atmosphere that simply reeks with class."

Perhaps the greatest vicarious thrill of such songs was the feeling of unfeeling. When *Top Hat* appeared in 1935, per capita personal income was $474 per year, and unemployment still hovered at 20 percent. The long queue at the soup kitchen—that abiding image of Depression-era urban destitution—was still not unknown in New York, Chicago, and other major cities; farmers fled prairie states that had become wind-whipped dust bowls. In this atmosphere, Americans couldn't help but lust for the extravagant detachment of Berlin's "No Strings" narrator, who boasts of having "No strings and no connections / No ties to my affections." In *Top Hat,* Astaire's Jerry Travers sings the song while idling in his London hotel suite; it is a rogue's ode to the single life, but above all a declaration of decadence: Travers's sole commitment is to the pursuit of high-toned pleasure. "I'm fancy free," he sings while spritzing soda water into a highball of bourbon, "And free for anything fancy."

The narrator of Berlin's "White Christmas" verse—that poor soul marooned in a Beverly Hills paradise—is recognizably a variation on that Astairean type: a blasé society swell. But by 1938, when Berlin was grappling with "White Christmas" and his various plans for a theatrical revue, history was catching up with popular culture's fancy-free cosmopolitans. While Roosevelt's New Deal reforms were lifting the nation from the depths of economic crisis, Americans were awakening to a different nightmare. Hitler was menacing Europe, Spain was rent by civil war, the Japanese were bombing Canton. In the shadow of geopolitical strife, the charm of penthouse pop was wearing off. Berlin's latest Astaire-Rogers vehicle arrived in cinemas that August under a title, *Carefree*, that felt unseemly—out of sync with a more solemn and engaged national mood.

This shift in public taste was underscored by the demise of Broadway and Hollywood's songwriting elite. On July 11, 1937, thirty-eight-year-old George Gershwin died, suddenly and shockingly, of a brain tumor. That same year, Cole Porter's legs were crushed in a horrible horseback-riding accident, a calamity from which his career would take years to recover. Lorenz Hart, the era's darkest and most debonair wit, sank deeper into alcoholism and self-destruction; soon his partner Richard Rodgers would find an earnest new collaborator, Oscar Hammerstein II, the author of odes to "Ol' Man River" and to cornstalks "as high as an elephant's eye." As the decade wound down, the eminence of Tin Pan Alley itself was under siege: for good-time musical diversion, American youth was increasingly turning to instrumental tunes played by swinging big bands.

Berlin foretold the twilight of this pop culture era in perhaps his greatest song of the 1930s, "Let's Face the Music and Dance," from the Astaire-Rogers picture *Follow the Fleet* (1936). Musically, the song finds Berlin at his stylish finest, its verses stepping ominously through a series of minor-chord changes whose elegance and menace recall the best Kurt Weill. The lyric is even more remarkable, distilling the wishing-the-world-away desperation behind those High Deco 1930s movies and pop songs. Over a brooding C minor vamp, "Let's Face the Music and Dance" begins with an indelible line: "There may be trouble ahead." Those words had dark resonance in 1936, the year that the Rome-Berlin Axis was proclaimed and

Franco launched his revolt against the Spanish Republic—
history was closing in on Hollywood's fairy tales of "moonlight
and music / And love and romance." In *Follow the Fleet,* the
song is staged as an archetypal expression of that fantasy:
Astaire sings the song in his usual black-tie resplendence,
while snaking Rogers around a gleaming Deco set. But as the
melody's foreboding downward tug suggests, the clock is tick-
ing on this dream; around the corner, he sings, there may be
"teardrops to shed." "Soon," Astaire sings, "We'll be . . . humming a diff'rent tune."

In the autumn of 1938, Berlin composed that tune.

He was in London, attending the British premiere of
Alexander's Ragtime Band. The film, a cheerful Berlin greatest-
hits package, was well received by British audiences and critics. But Berlin could scarcely take satisfaction in such
triumphs: Europe was girding for war. For months, tensions
had been mounting over Hitler's claims on Czech Sudetenland; in September 1938, Germany demanded annexation of
the territory. On September 29, the day before the *Alexander's
Ragtime Band* premiere, the Munich Pact was signed, authoriz-
ing Germany's partition of the Sudetenland—a last-ditch
attempt to head off war capped by British prime minister
Neville Chamberlain's famous forecast of "peace for our
time." Like most Americans, Berlin had followed the news in
recent months with growing disquiet; now, in England—separated from a besieged Europe by a mere twenty-one miles of
English Channel—the surreal newspaper headlines had a
terrifying immediacy. Chamberlain's assurances offered little
solace.

On the journey back to New York aboard the ocean liner *Normandie,* Berlin set to work on a new song. What he had in mind was a "peace song"—an anthem to soothe and reassure a jittery American public. He struggled to come up with the right tune, toying with a song entitled "Thanks, America" and another called "Let's Talk About Liberty." He had made several unsuccessful passes at the project before remembering a number he had abandoned more than two decades earlier: a few lines of purple patriotic verse, set to a martial A major melody, conceived in 1917 as a set piece for his World War I revue, *Yip Yip Yaphank.* The songwriter dragged out the old tune, changed a couple of lyrics, adjusted a musical phrase. Soon Berlin's revamped song was complete.

The result was a radical about-face from songs like "No Strings," "Top Hat, White Tie, and Tails," and the verse of the fledgling "White Christmas." Earnest where those songs were flippant and icily aloof, filled with pastoral images where those songs evoked big-city refinement, "God Bless America" was an anthem for a changing world. Berlin gave the song to Kate Smith, who specialized in large-lunged bombast and looked like a farmer's wife. She was the anti-Astaire.

Smith introduced "God Bless America" on her national radio broadcast on Armistice Day, November 11, 1938. Within days the song was everywhere: sung in churches, in ballparks, in public schools, at the White House, embraced by millions as an alternative national anthem to Francis Scott Key's unwieldy "The Star-Spangled Banner." This idea incensed nativists, who decried the "phony patriotism" of a tune that was, they hastened to point out, written by a "Russian," and for a time the merits of "God Bless America" became a topic of vehement editorial-page debate. But the song's critics were soon shouted down (what could be more patriotic, Berlin's defenders argued, than an immigrant's paean of praise to his adopted "home sweet home"?); and Berlin dealt the crackpots a killer blow by announcing that every cent of the song's royalties would be donated to the Boy and Girl Scouts of America.

It wasn't just the specter of world war that prompted the overwhelming response to "God Bless America." In the 1930s, the perennial American tension between progress and nostalgia was especially acute. The country was on the one hand in thrall to the modernity celebrated in, and embodied by, Tin Pan Alley's sleek, cosmopolitan songs. The census revealed that America was now an urban nation, and millions of new American city dwellers, émigrés from rural America and from overseas, reveled in the excitement of urban life. The increased cultural and political stature of cities, the impact of mass production and consumption, of progressive religious instruction in churches and scientific teaching in public schools, of radio, motion pictures, and other high-tech mass media—all these contributed to an atmosphere of bracing modernity, to the feeling that the nation was speeding headlong into a science-fiction future of limitless possibility and sophistication.

But the Depression made plain that technological revolution offered no guarantee of the good life. New urbanites confronted the anomie of city life, discovering that the fruits of modern, big-city individualism came at the expense of connection—the sense of security and stability that in the past had been provided by ancestral and communal ties. Even Tin

Pan Alley's inveterate New Yorkers registered this discontent; song after classic song features noirish, Hopperesque scenes of solitude and urban isolation, lonesome narrators pining for "someone to watch over me," stupefied by longing "In the roaring traffic's boom / In the silence of my lonely room."

As the thirties wore on, Americans felt increasing dissatisfaction with urban modernity—a sense that the country's best essence lay in its preindustrial past. Depictions of small-town simplicity and a utopian yesteryear became staples of popular culture. In WPA murals and Popular Front posters, farmers reaped the plenty of pastures bathed in golden light; small-town Regular Joes, good-hearted and full of American horse sense, strode through Thornton Wilder's theatrical smash *Our Town* (1938) and Frank Capra's films; Norman Rockwell's sentimental *Saturday Evening Post* cover illustrations depicted the wholesome procession along Main Street, USA. Commercial advertising was rife with images of nineteenth-century domestic harmony and agrarian life—Currier and Ives enlisted to sell breakfast cereal. Folkish imagery even penetrated such "high art" as the symphonic works of Aaron Copeland and the choreography of Martha Graham.

This pastoral nostalgia dovetailed with another popular preoccupation: rifling the back pages of history to discover the Truly American. Certainly, American historical self-consciousness was nothing new. But in the 1930s, with the trauma of the Depression and the menace of Nazism and other foreign ideologies deepening Americans' need for psychic reassurance, the quest to recover an organic national character became something of a crusade. The search for the "American way of life"—a phrase that, the cultural historian Warren Susman points out, first came into common use in the 1930s, along with such other telltale terms as "the American dream" and "the grass roots"—linked scholarly works like Constance Rourke's *American Humor: A Study in National Character* and Van Wyck Brooks's *The Flowering of New England* with grandiose projects like the Rockefeller-funded restoration of Colonial Williamsburg. The same impulse guided the efforts of so-called folk revivalists to document and preserve the country's indigenous song traditions. It was during the 1930s that John and Alan Lomax crisscrossed the rural United States, from New England to Appalachia to the Deep South, making thousands of recordings of ballads and blues and field hollers—the "authentic" music of the American folk.

Though these songs were absorbed into left-wing movements like the Popular Front, the ideology of the folk revival was as much aesthetic as political: behind its cult of authenticity was disdain for the artifice and schmaltz of Tin Pan Alley pop. The movement's torchbearer, Woody Guthrie, championed "people's ballads" as the earthy alternative to the Hit Parade's "sissy-voiced" crooners. When Guthrie wrote his most famous song, "This Land Is Your Land" (original title: "God Blessed America"), in response to Berlin's anthem, he was replying not just to the tune's jingoism but to the grandiose production values and bloated emotionalism of Kate Smith's ubiquitous recording. Guthrie and his fellow acoustic-guitar-wielding folkies stood for grit, homespun verities, unflinching realism; at the bottom of his "This Land Is Your Land" lyric sheet, Guthrie noted: "All you can write is what you see."

"God Bless America" may have been Guthrie's bête noire, but its images of "mountains . . . prairies . . . oceans white with foam" resonated with millions of listeners as an almost mystical evocation of the American landscape; in its skyward-striving strains, Berlin's mob heard a "people's ballad." An even greater Irving Berlin "folk anthem" lay in wait: that Christmas song he'd stuck in the trunk.

In the winter of 1939, when Berlin's thoughts were once again turning to "White Christmas," nostalgia for the rural past had overtaken popular culture. The year's top movie hits were a Civil War epic evoking the grandeur of the vanished South (*Gone With the Wind*), a musical about a Kansas farm girl who longs to return home (*The Wizard of Oz*), and the story of a political crusader striving to return the country to small-town values (*Mr. Smith Goes to Washington*). The year's literary sensation was *The Grapes of Wrath,* John Steinbeck's vision of vanishing agrarian utopia. The New York World's Fair was revamping its look, replacing the sci-fi "World of Tomorrow" with an overgrown county fair. Its new main attraction would be a stage spectacular called "American Jubilee," featuring rippling flags and cornball reenactments of the Gettysburg Address and other Great Historical Moments; its mascot, a folksy common man named Elmer.

When Berlin returned to "White Christmas" just after the New Year, he must have seen it with new eyes. We can imagine why. He'd begun the song as a genre parody, funning the sentimental ballad; now, with the country captivated by visions of yesteryear, his send-up was looking like the real article. It was a happy accident: the song's "dream" of an old-time

Christmas—Berlin's joke at the expense of Beverly Hills society—expressed a longing that was, seemingly, as ancient as the wintry New England landscape it evoked.

Helmy Kresa was unimpressed when Berlin showed up on January 8, 1940, announcing he'd written his greatest song. But he soon realized the songwriter wasn't blowing smoke. "When he sang the chorus," Kresa recalled, "I knew it really was the greatest song ever written. I was as thrilled as he was."

Today, "White Christmas" is so familiar that we hardly hear it. It has been "played so often," Alec Wilder reminds us, "that it is easy to forget . . . the truly daring succession of notes in the chromatic phrase of the [song's] main strain." Whatever emotions the song provokes—bemusement, annoyance, nostalgia for old times, foreboding about Christmas shopping still to be done—we can scarcely hope to relive the purity of Kresa's experience, when he heard it for the first time on a winter morning in an office building on Broadway.

The "White Christmas" chorus is in formal terms no different from thousands of Tin Pan Alley love ballads: thirty-two measures of music divided into four eight-bar sections. Lyrically, it is the epitome of Berlinian simplicity. Forty-four of its fifty-three words are monosyllables; its rhymes—snow/know; listen/glisten; write/bright/white—are rudimentary, almost banal. It is rhythmically unspectacular; in contrast to the verse, with its triplets and moments of light syncopation, the "White Christmas" chorus moves in steady, hymnlike flow. The movement of its melody is not, at first blush, terribly dramatic. The song generally stays within a single octave, briefly climbing above it twice and dropping below it once.

Yet we can appreciate what Helmy Kresa found so thrilling, for beneath the surface austerity of "White Christmas" there is plenitude, beauty, strangeness. Kresa transcribed literally hundreds of Irving Berlin songs. But the thirty-two bars of the "White Christmas" chorus stand as the single most elegant and economical marriage of music and words in a songwriting career dedicated to those virtues.

The chorus begins with a statement: "I'm dreaming." This declaration announces the song as a reverie. But who is dreaming, and where is he dreaming, and when? Berlin's verse provides definite answers: the dreamer is that East Coast exile, stuck in Beverly Hills, L.A., on Christmas Eve. But with the verse cropped from the song, our narrator becomes a more shadowy figure, a more vague and more universal dreamer: anyone singing the song or anyone hearing it; Bing Crosby, or Otis Redding, or you, or me.

The "White Christmas" stage set is spare. From the reference to writing Christmas cards we can infer that the date is sometime in December and the place is likely indoors. (Perhaps, as Mark W. Booth has suggested, the narrator sits in semidarkness, before "a window with no snow beyond it.") Even the pastoral landscape for which the narrator longs is only dimly sketched. Children stand in a snowy wood, listening for sleigh bells: this is the sum total of Berlin's "White Christmas" tableau.

These few images, though, are enough to conjure a familiar Christmas scene. We have stepped back in time, into a wintry New England landscape untouched by modernity. A cottage is tucked on a snow-shrouded hilltop. There must be a plume of smoke curling from a chimney, for inside the little house a hearth fire is surely aglow. Trees shimmer beneath a cold blue sky. A group of children, swaddled in scarves, stands listening for the faint tinkle of bells. Soon, a horse-drawn sleigh will come into view—no horseless carriages ply the roads of this distant century—wending its way up the hill.

This is a vision of Christmas as a sojourn in an idyllic American past. Berlin's Christmas is a sanctuary in time—an escape from the confusion of contemporary life to the rural yesteryear, to the embrace of family, to the warmth of home and hearth; in *Holiday Inn,* Crosby's Jim Hardy sings the song before a flickering log fire while snowflakes fall outside his window. "White Christmas" is pointedly not religious—no angels or wise men intrude on its pastoral scene—yet the holiday it describes is palpably sanctified: the unblemished whiteness of the Christmas snowfall is the whiteness of purity and perfection.

In short, the scene depicted in "White Christmas" is a Christmas cliché, and an audaciously kitschy one at that; seemingly the only element missing is Santa Claus, himself— and who knows, he might be pulling up any moment now behind the jingling reins of that sleigh. The song is filled with musical echoes of the hallowed Christmas past. As the musicologist Michael Beckerman has pointed out, the surging, eight-note rise and fall that accompanies the phrase "Just like the ones I used to know" could easily "have come out of an eighteenth-century Christmas concerto," and the harmony that appears in the fifteenth and sixteenth measures ("To hear sleighbells in the snow") is identical to one in "Jingle Bells":

"In a one-horse open sleigh (hey!)." Another musical model is "Silent Night." The serenity and stillness of the "White Christmas" tableau recalls the famous hymn ("All is calm, all is bright"). And Berlin's concluding couplet ("May your days be merry and bright / And may all your Christmases be white")—ostensibly the phrase that the narrator inscribes in his Christmas cards—sounds like nothing so much as churchy benediction, Berlin's variation on "Sleep in heavenly peace."

But "White Christmas" is more than just a pastiche of hoary yuletide imagery and musical motifs: sadness creeps into this Christmas vision. Listen to the song's opening passage, "I'm dreaming of a white Christmas." The "daring" chromaticism to which Wilder refers is found here, in a melody that makes an eight-note Russian hat dance between E and G major. We are so accustomed to hearing this music that we might not perceive its exotic, brooding quality; plus, Crosby's languid "White Christmas" performances tend to elide some of the melody's stranger half-step movements. But there is no mistaking the darkness that envelops the rather tortuous three-note ascent through the title phrase ("white Christ-mas") in bar four.

Listening to "White Christmas," we sense the songwriter groping his way along the keyboard, feeling his way through the melody, guided by intuition. Berlin was, of course, a famously self-taught musician, so well known for his technical ineptitude that a favorite Tin Pan Alley sport found Berlin's colleagues competing to imitate the great man's stuttering piano style.

But Berlin's limitations worked to his advantage. Like so

many great musical autodidacts—the Beatles come to mind—
Berlin routinely flouted "rules" he didn't know existed; asked
once how greater technical knowledge would impact his songwriting, Berlin answered: "Ruin it." His songs are filled with
unorthodoxies whose beauty and originality startled the tech-
nically astute. And as is so often the case with Berlin, in
"White Christmas" the idiosyncrasies cohere into a whole that
feels both strange and inevitable, as if the songwriter plucked
a song that always existed from the ether.

The key musical passage in "White Christmas," in the
song's final eight-bar section, is a typical Berlin epiphany. The
tension that has been mounting throughout the song builds to
a breaking point in bars twenty-five, twenty-six, and twenty-
seven ("May your days be merry"). And then comes the cli-
max: the leap to the word "bright," the only word in the lyric
that is held for longer than four beats.

But the music that surrounds that key word, "bright," is
the opposite of what we would expect. A momentary dissonance is introduced on the first beat of that twenty-eighth
measure. The dissonance quickly resolves, but more shadows
gather when, over the second half of the held note "bright,"
the chord shifts from F major to minor. This climactic passage
is followed by a kind of spooky coda, with its own musical
shocks: the appearance of a suave diminished G chord in the
twenty-ninth measure; and the surprising dip below the middle C that accompanies the final phrase "Christmases be
white."

How do we explain the gloominess of this key "White
Christmas" passage—that Christmas "brightness" that turns

so dark? We must return to the song's frame narrative, and to that ghostly figure, the lone dreamer. He sits dolefully in the (snowless) present, pining for the Christmases he *used* to know. The holiday wonder that the song describes is conspicuously and hopelessly out of his reach. "What is 'White Christmas,' " Michael Beckerman asks, "but a kind of holiday *Moby-Dick*, a distant image of things that can never be reclaimed: the past, childhood, and innocence itself?" The world's favorite Christmas song is not an ode to joy, or snowmen, or Santa. It is a downer, a lament for lost happiness—in spirit, if not in form, a blues.

It is difficult to resist the urge to search for autobiographical resonance in Berlin's brooding carol. It is hard not to imagine, as several commentators have, that the song's wistful narrator did not in some way give voice to a Jewish immigrant's feelings of estrangement from the Christian festival. (Mary Ellin Barrett remembers her father's seeming aloofness at his family's holiday celebrations: "in spirit," she says, he was still a "quizzical . . . vistor" at Christmastime.)

But of course, the songwriter had a more personal source of Christmas melancholy: the Yahrzeit of his only son. Berlin had a habit of marking pivotal moments in his life with special songs. "When I Lost You" was his widower's requiem for his first wife, Dorothy Goetz. "Always" was his wedding gift to Ellin. "Blue Skies," written in the weeks after the birth of his first child, was, according to Berlin, "for Mary Ellin, her song." Might "White Christmas" also be a song in this private tradition—a quiet lament for the ghost that haunted Berlin's Christmas past?

* * *

In April of 1940, three months after he brought the song to Kresa, nearly two years after he'd first started toying with ideas for stage revues, Berlin at last found a venue for his Christmas song. While in Washington, D.C., for a film premiere, the songwriter bumped into Mark Sandrich, one of Hollywood's leading directors. Sandrich, a handsome forty-year-old with startling deep-set dark eyes, had directed three Berlin pictures, *Top Hat, Follow the Fleet,* and *Carefree.* Now, the songwriter had a scheme for a new film. Berlin insisted that they decamp to a nearby diner to discuss it.

Over coffee, Berlin revealed his idea: a movie about a star singer who retires to the country to run a hotel open only on holidays. Berlin's outline of the plot was vague; but as both men knew, the purpose of a movie musical plot was to agreeably mark time between explosions of singing and hoofing, and Berlin's idea for a film of original holiday tunes was, Sandrich agreed, a winning gimmick. What's more, Berlin had already gotten a head start writing some of the numbers, he told Sandrich: he'd been batting around a similar idea for a Broadway show for a while now.

The pair parted with a handshake agreement to undertake the project. Over the next several months, in a slew of phone calls, cables, and face-to-face meetings, a deal was hammered out. By September, it was all but official: Mark Sandrich would direct the new Irving Berlin musical for Paramount Pictures. The film's working title was *Holiday Inn.*

For almost nine months, "White Christmas" had been

tucked away—a secret song that Berlin had shared only with Kresa. We can picture a prideful paternal gleam in the songwriter's eye when he wrote to his lawyer George Cohen on September 3, 1940, about his plans for *Holiday Inn*: "There is already one song done for the picture. It is called WHITE CHRISTMAS and it is to be a main part of the contract."

5

Good Jewish Music

Songwriters' Row: Tin Pan Alley circa 1914.
Courtesy of The Irving Berlin Music Company.

Everyone should have a Lower East Side in their lives.

—IRVING BERLIN

You swore that you would,
So be true to your vow:
Let's all be Americans now.

—IRVING BERLIN,
"Let's All Be Americans Now"

THERE IS A FAMOUS anecdote about Oscar Hammerstein II and Jerome Kern discussing plans for a musical based on Donn Byrne's *Messer Marco Polo.* "Here is a story," Hammerstein said, "laid in China about an Italian and told by an Irishman. What kind of music are you going to write?" Kern replied: "It'll be good Jewish music."

The incident may be apocryphal, but that borscht-belt-worthy punch line rings true. In the first half of the twentieth century, what American pop music *wasn't* Jewish? A generation before Adolph Zukor, William Fox, Louis B. Mayer, and Benjamin Warner founded Hollywood, another group of Jewish strivers invented popular music as a mass medium, turning the sale of sheet music from a ragtag cottage industry into a billion-dollar business. The creative end of the pop song business was dominated by Jewish songwriters: Eastern European Jewish immigrants like Irving Berlin, and second-generation Jewish-Americans like Kern. In the ranks of the era's greatest composers there numbered only one gentile, Cole Porter—an ardent philo-Semite who once announced he had discovered the secret to songwriting success: "write Jewish tunes."

The story of these Jewish music makers and moguls is one of the most piquant in American popular culture. It still seems remarkable that the body of tunes we regard as the essence of musical Yankee Doodle—"Alexander's Ragtime Band," "Tea for Two," "Blue Skies," "Blue Moon," "I Got Rhythm," "I've Got the World on a String," "Ol' Man River," "Stormy Weather," "As Time Goes By," "'S Wonderful," "Over the Rainbow," to name just a handful—was largely the creation of men and women just a step or two removed from the cities and shtetlach of the Pale of Settlement. That feat led one leading historian to dub Broadway "the epicenter of American Jewish culture."

But while Berlin, Kern, Gershwin, and company have been enshrined in Jewish-American history, the very "Jewishness" of their accomplishment remains vague. What exactly is *Jewish* about Tin Pan Alley's "good Jewish music"?

Cole Porter had his ideas. Porter's "Jewish tunes"—"Night and Day," "Begin the Beguine," "Love for Sale"—moved mournfully through chromatic passages whose midnight-in-the-Casbah exoticism reminds us of a time when Jews were still regarded as "Orientals." Porter was not alone in invoking what might be called racial musical stereotypes. Many observers have detected in the minor-key dolor of certain ballads a timeless Jewish melancholy—generations of cantors sobbing behind the strains of "My Funny Valentine" and "Summertime." The English composer and critic Constant Lambert called Tin Pan Alley "a commercialized Wailing Wall"; Berlin's first biographer, the drama critic and Algonquin Roundtable fixture Alexander Woollcott, breathlessly wrote of the magic by which the songwriter "transmuted into music the jumbled sounds of his life":

> The cries of the fruit vendors and the push cart peddlers, the chants in the synagogues . . . above all, the plaintive race notes, the wail of his sorrowing tribe, the lamentation of a people harried and self-pitying since time out of mind.

But others have dismissed altogether the Jewishness of American song standards. Writing in 1929, the great historian of Jewish music Abraham Idelsohn found in the songs of Berlin and Gershwin "not a single element that bears Jewish features or that might be reckoned as a distinctly Jewish contribution. . . . There is no standard or measure by which we can distinguish . . . a jazz song by Irving Berlin from the other innumerable modern Anglo-Saxon popular 'hits.' " More recently, the Brill Building songwriters Mike Leiber and Jerry Stoller—Jews themselves—scorned as "hogwash" the notion that "Irving Berlin's Jewishness influenced his writing of 'White Christmas.' "

Indeed, "White Christmas" would seem to be the glaring case that proves the point. Even Woollcott, had he lived long enough to hear it, would have had difficulty detecting "plaintive race notes" in Berlin's Christmas tune. The ethnicity of its creator is, seemingly, the only thing remotely Jewish about the song; and from the moment he fled his Orthodox home at age thirteen, Berlin's Jewish affiliation was dubious. Isn't it a stretch to search for Yiddishkeit in a yuletide carol?

In fact, it is the patent non-Jewishness of "White Christmas" that makes it the archetypal creation of Jewish Tin Pan Alley. The "good Jewish music" of the song-standard era is a sound track of assimilation, the musical record of a marginalized people's conquest of the cultural mainstream. Like their Hollywood cousins, the Jews of Tin Pan Alley were outsiders skilled at recognizing the desires of the American middle class they strove to enter. They specialized in the cultural sleight of hand that Kern winked at in his *Messer Marco Polo* quip: distilling a variety of influences, archetypes, and musical motifs into a distinct concoction, which they sold back to America as homegrown music.

This process was largely unconscious, but as Kern's quote reveals, the Jews of Tin Pan Alley and Broadway had a sly awareness that in creating the nation's pop music a type of cultural manipulation was at work. "What care I who makes the laws of a nation," Berlin wrote in "Let Me Sing and I'm Happy" (1928), "As long as I can sing its popular songs." It was not an empty boast: at a time when Jews were still marginalized socially and politically, their dominance of mass entertainment put them at the forefront of an industry that had unprecedented power to shape popular ideas about what was American. Jews seized that power with gusto and, in so doing, not only helped refashion Jewish identity but, in ways large and small, refashioned the country—turned their American dreams into an alluring version of *the* American dream.

"White Christmas" is an abiding symbol of that accomplishment, and it is tempting to read Berlin's life, and the larger pop culture movement he spearheaded, as a trajectory arcing toward the song; the crusade that began in the rowdy musical melting pot of the Lower East Side climaxed three decades later with a Christmas ode delivered in the ethnically homogenized voice of the American Everyman. The commercial pinnacle of the golden age of popular song, a collaboration between its definitive songwriter and singer, "White Christmas" also embodied the era's secret theme: pop music as the fulfillment of Jewish-American destiny—musical alchemy that transmuted Jewish otherness into generic Americanness. Berlin was asked how "a member of the Jewish faith" could write "White Christmas." "I know how," he said in a 1954 interview. "I wrote it as an American."

Irving Berlin's storied American life began in classic American fashion: on a continent half a world away. The "Jewboy who named himself after an English actor and a German city," as George M. Cohan quipped, was born Israel Baline, in 1888, possibly on May 11, probably in Tyumen, a bleak town on the banks of the Tura River in western Siberia. The youngest child of Moses Baline, a cantor, arrived at a desperate moment for the Jews of the Russian empire, who were scourged by poverty and lived in constant fear of pogroms, the murderous raids on Jewish enclaves that became widespread following the assassination of Tsar Alexander II in 1881. When Israel was four or five years old, rampaging *pogromniks* arrived in his village; his earliest childhood memory was of huddling with his mother, Leah, and watching the family home burn to the ground. Such mob attacks often coincided with Christian holidays, when Russian peasants, drunk on liquor and anti-Judaic theology, turned against their Jewish neighbors. Though the date of the pogrom that left the Balines homeless is unsure, it is a virtual certainty that, in the frigid Siberian winters of his early childhood, the composer of that rhapsody to yuletides "just like the ones I used to know" first experienced Christmas as a day of dread.

Berlin's early life traced a fabled route. A steerage-class journey aboard the ocean liner SS *Rhynland* carried Israel, his five sisters, his older brother, and their parents to Ellis Island on September 11, 1893. The Balines were part of the massive emigration that brought 20 million Eastern and Southern Europeans into the United States in the years between 1870 and 1915. The family settled into that teeming immigrant epicenter, the Lower East Side, which by the 1890s was already among the most densely populated places on earth, with over one thousand inhabitants per acre. Elbowroom was scarce in their new home, a tenement apartment at 330 Cherry Street: four tiny rooms for eight Balines.

Israel arrived in a bewildering environment of brash colors and bustling streets as an archetypal "greenhorn": a Yiddish-speaking child in an ill-fitting suit of old-world clothes. His parents never really recovered from the ordeal of their dislocation. Leah Baline lived in the United States nearly thirty years but at the time of her death spoke only a few words of English. Cantor Baline worked as a kosher meat inspector and took other menial jobs; he contracted chronic bronchitis and died in 1901, at the age of fifty-three. Israel, though, adapted quickly. By the time he was a seven-year-old second-grader at P.S. 20 on Monroe Street—where his teacher complained "he just dreams and sings to himself"—he had a newsie's tweed hat, a command of off-color slang, and a jaunty American nickname, Izzy.

"Everyone should have a Lower East Side in their lives," Berlin was fond of saying, and it wasn't just a hard-boiled pose—a millionaire gruffly remembering the slums. In the fun-house-mirror world of popular song, this was more or less a statement of fact. Tin Pan Alley was overrun with Lower East Side natives, whose hardscrabble childhoods seemed to give them a leg up in a trade defined by hustle and a streetwise feel for mass taste. The idea of the Lower East Side as a kind of mystical breeding ground of Jewish greatness still has nostalgic currency in the twenty-first century; at the height of Jewish domination of American popular music, the notion was, for some, almost oppressively real. "Had I been born on the Lower East Side," Cole Porter told Sammy Cahn, "I might have been a true genius."

We may chuckle at Porter, the blue blood who sang the glories of intercontinental high life, cursing the fate that denied him a ghetto childhood. But there was something to his theory. The sons and daughters of the Lower East Side and other

Jewish immigrant centers—Philadelphia's West End, Boston's North End, Chicago's South Side, West Detroit—were heirs to a cultural tradition whose expressiveness made them emotionally well suited to the task of writing popular songs. They had the good fortune to arrive in America at the moment when, and to settle in the places where, the pop song was being turned into a mass medium. And if the Lower East Side wasn't quite the seething bazaar that Alexander Woollcott imagined, Porter was right to suppose that his "true geniuses" grew up in a musical environment a good deal more vibrant than what he experienced in his midwestern boyhood.

On Lower East Side street corners, buskers sang the latest popular tunes, organ grinders plied, venders hawked sheet music. The neighborhood's broader thoroughfares were lined with music stores and music halls, which ranged from gutbucket burlesque houses and variety theaters—of both the English- and Yiddish-language types—to more upscale, "legitimate" theaters. Scarcely a Lower East Side block was without a storefront "dancing academy," where young Jews went to learn the latest steps and flirt. The sounds of merry, lowbrow songs poured out of the dives and dance halls along the Bowery. At East Side weddings, guests were regaled with Jewish music that ran the spectrum from sacred (the solemn prayers intoned by the cantor during the nuptial ceremony) to secular (the freewheeling klezmer music that propelled celebratory dancing) to borderline profane (the frequently bawdy improvised rhymes sung by the *badchen,* or wedding jester). And there were "the chants in the synagogues": ancient liturgical melodies that resonated in what were, at the turn of the century, hundreds of makeshift shuls packed into the Lower East Side's twelve square miles.

The vivacious musical scene on the Lower East Side reflected the richness of the musical traditions that Ashkenazic Jews brought to America from Eastern Europe. Today, when our vision of the lost universe of Eastern European Jewry is dominated by images of folksiness, piety, and suffering, we might picture scenes of old-world Jewish music-making out of Chagall, or Bock and Harnick: bearded fiddlers perched on, or floating beatifically above, shtetl rooftops. But the reality of Jewish life in Eastern Europe was complex, and Jewish musical culture was no exception—eclectic, cosmopolitan, and influenced by contact with non-Jewish music.

One tradition stands out as a precursor to the "good Jewish music" of Tin Pan Alley: Yiddish folk song. In the mid–nineteenth century, as the influence of the Haskalah, or Jewish enlightenment movement, spread to the Pale of Settlement from the cities of Western Europe, the political and cultural life of East European Jewry was infused with an urbane spirit. Jewish writers devoted themselves to developing the Yiddish vernacular, long scorned as lowly "jargon," into a medium of artistic expression. The resulting literary ferment—the classic Yiddish fiction of S. Y. Abramovitsh, Sholem Aleichem, and I. L. Peretz—is much celebrated. But Yiddish-language song also flourished, as minstrels set Yiddish texts to tunes based on liturgy, folk tradition, or borrowed from non-Jewish sources. Encompassing all aspects of Jewish life—large and small, domestic and political—these songs appealed especially to less educated and less affluent Jews, for whom they served as not only entertainment but sources of information about the rapidly changing social landscape of the Jewish world. Significantly, the massive movement of Jews to the United States during the latter part of the century gave rise to a whole genre of Yiddish songs about America and the immigrant experience. Before they even reached the New World, the relationship of millions of Jews to the United States was being expressed through the medium of popular song.

Jews were hardly the only immigrants to bring a festive musical culture to their new American home. What distinguished them from other immigrant groups was the passion with which they embraced music as a vocation. The terrific striving of Jewish immigrants—the emphasis they placed on education and the tenacity with which they sought middle-class American lives—is a historical cliché. Less known is the fervor with which Jews channeled that energy into musical activity—their belief that music offered a way into the American economic mainstream. It was a lesson Jews had learned in the old country, where they had watched with awe the journeys of young violin and piano virtuosos, whose musical skills carried them from the Pale of Settlement to acclaim and prosperity in the concert halls of Western Europe.

Jewish parents made great sacrifices to give their children musical educations. "The whole neighborhood is teeming with young artists," wrote one Lower East Side social worker in 1906. "There is not a house, no matter how poor it be, where there is not . . . a piano or a violin, and where the hope of the whole family is not pinned on one of the younger set as a future genius."

Harry Ruby, a child of the Lower East Side who became a Tin Pan Alley legend, composing such hits as "Three Little Words," "I Wanna Be Loved by You," and "Who's Sorry Now?" told a similar story. Jewish parents, he recalled, "who barely had enough to eat and pay the rent—for some reason they wanted their children to learn [a musical instrument]. Everybody got lessons, in the hope that it would lead to something." Sammy Cahn was more succinct: "I was born into the typical Lower East Side Jewish family, in 1913. My mother insisted that I would play the violin."

The favorite instrument of Lower East Side mothers, however, was the piano. Among the Euro-American bourgeoisie, the instrument had long been regarded as a symbol of respectability, domesticity, and musical refinement—the crown jewel in the parlor of a proper middle-class home. Jewish immigrants, acutely interested both in music and in attaining the comforts and status of American middle-class life, embraced this icon with particular ardor. The peak years of piano production in the United States, the two decades between 1890 and 1910, coincided exactly with the height of the Jewish migration from Eastern Europe; hundreds of thousands of pianos were factory-built annually, at a rate that bested that of the nation's population growth by more than five times. The increased supply brought piano prices down, and installment-plan purchases of the instrument were introduced. With as small a down payment as $5, Jewish immigrants could take home what had formerly seemed an unattainable luxury item—an emblem of their elevated social position in the New World, and a symbol of hope for their children's American futures.

Each era in American popular music has seen the domin-
ion of a different musical instrument. The guitar did double
duty as rock 'n' roll's great style icon and supplier of its definitive sound; in the current postrock era of hip-hop and elec-
tronic dance music, guitars have given way to sequencers and
beat boxes. The first half of the twentieth century was pop's
piano era, and the cult of the piano among Jewish immigrants
offers one explanation for the Jews' peculiar success in popular song. Sophie Tucker, vaudeville's zaftig "Last of the Red
Hot Mamas," got her start in music when her parents bought
her a $25 secondhand baby grand piano, which they set up in
the front room directly above the restaurant they owned in
Hartford, Connecticut. A $5 used piano was the centerpiece of
the Lower East Side tenement where the young Irving Caesar
lived with his parents, siblings, and "six or seven lodgers." By
day, Caesar—who grew up to write the lyrics to "Tea for Two,"
"Crazy Rhythm," "Swanee," and other hits—took 25¢ piano
lessons from a local baker's daughter. At night, Caesar
recalled, "the piano turned into one of those early double-deck
bed effects. Two of us slept on top of it, and three of us slept
under it."

The Caesars' piano-cum-bunk-bed had been hoisted into
their tiny apartment on ropes, through the second-floor window. It was a ritual well-known in Jewish neighborhoods like
the Lower East Side; Harry Ruby remembers seeing an
upright piano lifted in this fashion into the apartment of his
Eldridge Street neighbors, the Gershwins. The spectacle of a
piano ascending a tenement facade would invariably draw a
crowd of gawkers on the street below, and seems a wonderful

metaphor for the high hopes and terrific determination that Jewish immigrants attached to their musical endeavors.

The success that Berlin and his fellow Lower East Siders found in popular music may, in the main, have been a matter of economics. In the first quarter of the century, prejudice and poverty placed stringent restrictions on Jewish social mobility; even the wealthiest and best-educated Jews found themselves frozen out of the professions. Music—in particular the "lower" forms of popular music, regarded by polite society as disreputable—was a field open to Jews when others were emphatically closed. The Lower East Siders whom Porter envied came to Tin Pan Alley in such overwhelming numbers because, unlike him, they had few other attractive options.

Still, the extraordinary Jewish achievement in American popular music suggests that, for many Jews, music had special allure. Music offered Jews something more than simple assimilation into the broader American mainstream: the chance to effect a cultural synthesis—a *Jewish* American identity. This is the idea behind two seminal works of twentieth-century American popular culture, Israel Zangwill's *The Melting Pot*—the play that put that phrase into the vernacular—and the film *The Jazz Singer,* both of which tell stories of Jewish immigrants creating their American selves through spectacular musical endeavor.

The Jazz Singer's tale of Jack Robin, the cantor's son who forsakes the synagogue for the glory of the vaudeville stage, is an especially interesting case. Al Jolson, the film's star, was in real life the son of a cantor, as were several of Tin Pan Alley's finest: Jay Gorney, Sammy Cahn, Harold Arlen, Yip Harburg.

This continuum of Jewish musical accomplishment across generations suggests a parallel with the great church-reared African-American singers—Ray Charles, Aretha Franklin, Sam Cooke, James Brown, to name just the most illustrious— who reinvented sacred gospel music as secular soul and R&B. Like those innovators, Jews found in music a means to access the American mainstream and reap its economic rewards while smuggling bits of their culture along for the ride. Al Jolson may have left his father's synagogue behind, but no one who ever watched him drop to his bended knees, fling his arms open, and belt out "My Mammy" could doubt that he had brought the trademark cantorial "tear in the voice"—and a dollop of Jewish schmaltz—with him.

Izzy Baline, the cantor's son who would grow up to write several of Jolson's signature numbers, dropped out of school when he was twelve years old to work full-time selling the William Randolph Hearst scandal sheet the *Evening Journal*. A year later, his father died. Shortly thereafter, Izzy left home. He went, Irving Berlin would recall later, "on the bum"—a period phrase that captures the hard-knock life he undertook, trading in the cot he shared with his brother, Benjamin, for park benches, tenement vestibules, and when he was lucky, 15¢-a-night Bowery lodging houses. Plunging into a new life in the lower Manhattan demimonde, the Russian bar mitzvah boy baptized himself an American. When he signed flophouse guest registers, it was not with his given Jewish name or its quasi-Americanized variant but the first of his pseudonyms: Cooney. When he awoke each day, he went to work as a singer of American popular songs.

Irving Berlin's teenage years on the roughhouse fringes of the music industry are a colorful part of his legend. He had a reedy tenor voice, not a subtle instrument but an effective one; as a newspaper boy, he had boosted sales—and earned the occasional tip—by crooning vaudeville hits for his customers. Now he had decided to make "busking" his full-time job. For the next two years, he roamed the Bowery, one of scores of teenage buskers who sang for spare change on street corners and in grimy beer houses with foreboding names: the Bucket of Blood, Suicide Hall.

Eventually, he found a steady job as a singing waiter at the Pelham Café in Chinatown. It was not a high-toned establishment. The Pelham's owner was "Nigger Mike" Salter, a Russian Jew with a swarthy complexion who claimed to have killed ten men; its square-jawed regulars included members of local Irish, Italian, and Jewish gangs. But the Pelham gave Izzy his first lyric-writing experience, concocting bawdy "blue" parodies of current hits, and it had a house piano. After hours, the teenager taught himself to pick out tunes.

At the same time that Izzy was first stalking the Bowery singing "sob ballads," American pop music was being transformed by a group of upstart Jewish entrepreneurs who brought brisk modern efficiency and promotional savvy to the production and marketing of songs. Most of the new song-publishing firms were clustered on a single noisy block of West Twenty-eighth Street in Manhattan, where the sound of ill-tuned pianos demonstrating new tunes could be heard day and night: Tin Pan Alley. This location put the song merchants in close contact with the New York–based variety and vaudeville entertainment syndicates, whose national touring troupes carried new tunes from Gotham to the provinces. A hit song in a vaudeville show could translate into thousands of sheet music sales; the publishers did all they could—bribing, cajoling, sweet-talking, arm-twisting—to get performers to feature their new tunes in acts.

Vaudevillians weren't the only focus of these "song plugging" efforts. Publishers' plugging staffs fanned out all over the city, undertaking stunts of all sorts to clobber new songs into public favor. They performed tunes on busy sidewalks, in beer gardens and amusement parks, at dime museums, in between reels at nickelodeons. They played them while wending through city streets, on pianos perched atop horse- and bicycle-drawn carts. Izzy Baline briefly found work as a "boomer" for the publishing house owned by songwriter Harry Von Tilzer. The teenager's job was to sit in a vaudeville balcony and, following a singer's performance of a new Von Tilzer tune, rise as if captivated by the song's majesty and reprise its chorus at the top of his lungs.

What really distinguished the new music publishers were the types of songs they sold. Old-guard publishing companies, such as the Boston-based firm of Oliver Ditson, had catalogs that included everything from piano-vocal scores of oratorios to church hymnals, and a highbrow mission to expose the public to the best of the Western musical tradition. The popular songs they published reflected a Victorian, Europhile sensibility: syrupy, "high-class" ballads that strove for the grandeur of Viennese light opera and narrated morality tales in high-flown diction.

By contrast, the new Jewish-owned, New York–based firms focused *exclusively* on popular tunes. This was a good quarter-century before the golden-age maturation of American pop. Still, the songs had charm. Their tunes had a native jollity; their lyrics reveled in the street-smart American vernacular in all of its punchiness and rude wit. The publishing houses churned out one song after another, aiming always at topicality, exploiting the latest public fancies and news events with tailor-written tunes. (One of the groundbreaking publishers hung a sign on his door: "Songs written to order.") The songs reflected New York's energy; its brashness; its obsession with commerce, new trends, and new technology; and above all its melting-pot demographics, which had transformed the city into a multi-ethnic spectacle whose like the world had never seen. A new century had begun, and New York was emerging as the country's cultural epicenter. Tin Pan Alley was supplying its invigorating sound track: spry, earthy songs—*American* music.

Izzy Baline's work as a singing waiter may not have been glamorous, but it put him at ground zero of the popular-song trade. By the time he turned nineteen, he was a six-year veteran of the song business. He had absorbed valuable lessons about the taste of the mob and how to put a tune over; he had performed nearly every Tin Pan Alley hit that had come down the pike—and "rewritten" many of them to suit the ribald taste of the Pelham Café's clientele.

That year, 1907, Izzy got a chance to put his lessons in this rough art to use. When the pianist at a rival saloon composed a hit "wop" song—a number written in crudely stereotypical "Italian dialect," the latest variation on the favorite Tin Pan

Alley game of ethnic caricature—Izzy's boss commanded the young waiter to collaborate with the house pianist on a response. The result, "Marie from Sunny Italy," was his first published song. It didn't earn him any real money (only 33¢); nor was it much of a song ("Please come out, tonight, my queen, / Can't you hear my mandolin?" went a typically inelegant couplet). But it was a foot in the door, and its sheet music rolled off the presses bearing a fateful typographical error: "Words by I. Berlin." Izzy Baline became "Irving Berlin," and never looked back.

Berlin's output from these early years is representative of the eclecticism of vaudeville-era music: a madcap mix of dance numbers, rakish novelty tunes, and above all, ethnic dialect songs: Jewish, Italian, Irish, German, and black parody tunes, written for vaudevillians who essayed those types in broad stage lampoons. The titles of Berlin's early songs evoke the freewheeling optimism of an America being transformed by its big cities, loosening morals, new immigrants, and new machines: "Keep Away from the Fellow Who Owns an Automobile," "Jake! Jake! The Yiddisher Ball-Player," "I Was Aviating Around," "Oh! Where Is My Wife To-Night?" "Sweet Marie, Make-a Rag-a-Time Dance Wid Me," "Abie Sings an Irish Song," "Colored Romeo," "Do Your Duty Doctor! (Oh, Oh, Oh, Oh, Doctor)," "The Elevator Man Going Up, Going Up, Going Up, Going Up!" But the song that launched Berlin's career into the stratosphere was "Alexander's Ragtime Band," Berlin's raucous 1911 hit that sold 2 million copies and established him as the country's songwriting superstar and "ragtime king."

Today, music historians dispute the legitimacy of Berlin's claim to that title. We understand that Tin Pan Alley's version of ragtime bore little resemblance to the complex syncopated music invented by Scott Joplin and other African-Americans— that Berlin the "ragtime king" was to Joplin as Elvis Presley "the king of rock 'n' roll" was to Little Richard, Chuck Berry, and other black musical pioneers of the late forties and early fifties.

But in the first two decades of the century, ragtime described something larger than a musical style. It was the attitude of the age, the progressive spirit of a polyglot, rapidly urbanizing nation loosing itself from its Victorian past and strutting into the classless future. For that ragtime zeitgeist, Berlin was as good a torchbearer as any. With their blunt, streetwise language and lively rhythms, his songs celebrated the exhilaration and erotic possibilities of life in the big city. Ragtime's rhythms and messages were, Berlin suggested, intoxicating, irresistible, medicinal. "Syncopation is the soul of every true American," he said. "Ragtime is the best heart-raiser and worry-banisher I know." In later years, Berlin changed a lyric in "Alexander's Ragtime Band" extolling music "So natural that you want to go to war" to the less belli-cose "So natural that you holler for more"; but the original line was apt. Ragtime was the sound of a country feeling its oats, and in the early 1910s, with Berlin scoring hits both at home and overseas, that infectious American sound seemed destined to conquer the world.

In any case, a ragtime war was already being fought on the domestic front. In the early twenty-first century, we can hardly imagine that Tin Pan Alley's ragtime tunes, with their rinky-dink piano sound and glad-hearted lyrical doggerel, packed the same subversive wallop as death metal or gangsta rap. But the history of popular music offers numerous examples of how time defangs the most menacing avant-gardes. Invariably, musical styles that emerge as revolutionary and outré are absorbed into mainstream culture: the Charlie Parker records that first struck listeners as an atonal maelstrom have become background music suitable for a cocktail lounge; the punk anthems that in the late 1970s promised anarchy and forecast "no future" have arrived in the future, after all—as the sound tracks to car commercials.

The commotion caused by ragtime in the first two decades of the century was, if anything, greater than any subsequent pop-inspired uproar. Musical educators scorned a public that was forsaking the Western classics for pop song "idiocy." Newspaper pundits thundered about the threat to public morality—especially, to the honor of young women—posed by the "suggestive" lyrics and manic rhythms emerging from New York's song factories. In October 1911, when "Alexander's Ragtime Band" was sweeping the nation, a prominent doctor told a Los Angeles audience that America was "being driven crazy by its ragtime music."

Ragtime is mainly responsible for many business failures and cases of hopeless insanity. Your ragtime air jars the nervecenters and causes an irritation of the brain cells. While the roll and thump of ragtime is exhilarating to the senses and acts as a stimulant, it has the after effects of an injurious drug that will eventually stagnate the brain cells and wreck the nervous system.

Lurking just beneath the surface of such hysteria was the Anglo-American majority's fear of miscegenation, cultural and otherwise. Suddenly, middle-class Americans were dancing to "Negro jungle rhythms" in tunes written by Jewish composers. "Everybody's Doin' It Now," crowed a Berlin hit of 1911, a claim made all the more unnerving by the fact that that titular "It" was left mischievously ill defined. Some of the first folk-music revivals date from this period, sponsored not by scholars or lefties but by wealthy nativists, bolstering the imperiled indigenous culture against the toxic spread of "Hebrew Broadway jazz."

In this heated environment, Berlin's "ragtime king" status identified him as a cultural renegade, but he managed, through sheer likability and careful milking of his Horatio Alger success story, to endear himself even to ragtime's opponents. For Americans of the Progressive Era, when a nervous nation struggled with the question of how to absorb its millions of new citizens, Berlin's rags-to-riches picaresque was irresistible. Newspapers from coast to coast hailed the wiry, mop-haired immigrant as the living embodiment of the American dream, the guttersnipe who rose from the slums to become a skyscraper-dwelling millionaire; as early as 1915, columnists were suggesting that the songwriter's life be made into a movie. (Berlin would spurn many Hollywood advances over the years.) But the melting-pot fable trumpeted in the media told only half the story. The nation was meeting its young troubadour halfway: Berlin had become American; America, in turn, was becoming Berlinian, embracing songs that enshrined an aggressively post-Victorian sensibility.

By the time that American "doughboys" marched off to World War I, Berlin had seemingly won over the last of his critics. In the spring of 1918, Berlin was drafted into military service; in August of that same year, he arrived on Broadway with a war-themed revue, *Yip Yip Yaphank,* starring a cast of his fellow soldiers. Now the nation's unofficial head cheerleader, recognized around the world as his young country's jolly musical ambassasor, he had only officially become an American citizen a few months earlier. One of his minor World War I hits was perhaps a commemoration of that milestone, but its title is as good a summary as any of the spirit behind his life's songwriting work: "Let's All Be Americans Now."

The United States emerged from the Great War a cocksure nation poised to claim its place of preeminence in the West. European economies had been decimated by the war, but America's was churning into a period of unprecedented expansion and prosperity. While the country flexed its new economic and political muscle, it was shrugging off its sense of cultural inferiority. It had begun producing its own vigorous and distinctive modern art, and none was more brilliant, or more robustly American, than its homegrown music: it was not for nothing that the "roaring" decade between the Great War and the Great Crash was known as the Jazz Age.

The American musical revolution of the 1920s was centered on two New York fronts, led by two groups of artistically trenchant arrivistes. Uptown, Duke Ellington, Fletcher Henderson, Fats Waller, Bessie Smith, and other jazz and blues innovators brought an urbane gleam to the vernacular musical traditions of African-Americans. On Broadway and Tin Pan Alley, a new generation of young songwriters, most of them Jews, infused popular song with similar energy, ambition, and polish. By the middle of the decade, ragtime tunes had given way to a more refined type of song: those lustrous thirty-two-bar variations on the theme "I love you." The popsong Golden Age was under way.

In artistic terms, the difference between ragtime songs and the witty, elegant ballads of the postwar period was unmistakable; the most telling change, however, was Tin Pan Alley's retreat from crazy-quilt topicality to a near-complete focus on romance. Gone were the songs about dance crazes, politics, rubes adrift in the city, immigrants, automobiles; gone were "Take Me Out to the Ballgame," "Come, Josephine in My Flying Machine," "The Chicken Reel," "Ragtime Cowboy Joe," "Chinatown, My Chinatown." Never before or since has there been as abrupt a change in the subject matter of American pop songs; there was far greater continuity, for instance, between the lyrical preoccupations of the earliest rock 'n' roll hits and the Golden Age songs that preceded them than there was between a Berlin song like "Don't Send Me Back to Petrograd"—a raucous dialect number sung in a heavy Russian accent by Fanny Brice in the Music Box Revue of 1924—and the quiet rumination of his big ballad hits of 1925 and 1926, "Remember" and "Always."

The change in song style can be ascribed to a range of factors: to the organic ebb and flow of public taste; to the rise of phonograph records, commercial radio, and other technologies that fostered more intimate, inward-focused music; to the demise of vaudeville and arrival of a slicker, "uptown" brand of musical theater that demanded more genteel songs.

But the advent of the Golden Age love ballad also bears on American popular song's "Jewish question." The Great War stimulated a deep mistrust of foreigners and spurred a rise in xenophobic prejudice against "hyphenated" Americans, a trend dramatically illustrated by the postwar Red scares and the resurgence of a reinvigorated Ku Klux Klan. In 1917, under intense pressure from the Immigration Restriction League and other nativist groups, Congress had enacted a law requiring immigrants over the age of sixteen to pass a literacy test to be admitted to the United States. This was followed, in 1921 and 1924, by legislation that set quotas drastically reducing the numbers of immigrants from such areas as Eastern and Southern Europe. Between 1924 and 1947, only 2.7 million immigrants came to the United States, a total equal to the number entering the country during any two-year period prior to the First World War; in the 1930s, the number of those who left the United States outnumbered those who immigrated for the first time in the nation's history.

This mood of heightened nativism registered in the disappearance from pop music of that cacophony of ethnically inflected voices. Although the ethnic characters that populated ragtime-era pop songs were often stereotyped grotesques, the cumulative effect of so many songs in so many different voices was to exalt and celebrate urban America's polyglot pageant. In a postwar climate hostile to the dramatization of ethnic difference, Tin Pan Alley muzzled its accents; the implied protagonist of Golden Age love songs was almost always a generic white American. It was no coincidence that after the First World War, the fervent Jewish belters (Jolson, Tucker, Brice, Belle Baker) who had dominated pop singing were gradually replaced by a new breed of All-American smoothies (Crosby, Astaire, Rudy Vallée), whose crooning projected postethnic ease and reserve.

But from the distance of decades, the ethnic erasure in the pop songs of the Golden Age looks less like capitulation than wish fulfillment. For at the center of the American Songbook there stands a modest and majestic Jewish invention: the Regular Guy. He is a figure we know well: that wisecracking but ultimately good-hearted fellow who, disguised variously as Jimmy Cagney and Jimmy Stewart and Bing Crosby and Frank Sinatra, strode with a snap-brimmed hat and a loose-limbed gait through the popular culture of the American midcentury. Whether exulting in "I've Got the World on a String," brooding in "Glad to Be Unhappy," declaring his love in "Always," or weeping in his drink in "But Not for Me," he spoke from a perfect and perfectly imaginary place—a spiritual, if not geographic, heartland—in an accent whose jocularity hinted at an ethnic past but which was triumphantly post-melting-pot all-American.

This Everyman character is unmistakably a projection of Jewish desire: a fantasy self-image stamped in song and celluloid. He is upwardly mobile. He has traces of ethnicity, but the rough edges have been smoothed out. He has downtown street smarts but uptown "class." In short, he resembles no one so much as those members of the up-from-Hester-Street show business mafia that created him in the first place.

That such a broad cross section of Americans embraced with such fervor the "Jewish tunes" that he inhabited shows that the desires of Jews—their yearning for belonging and for the emotional and material comforts of middle-class life—mirrored those of the population at large. During the turbulent decade and a half that stretched from the stock market crash through the Second World War, when adversity united the country as never before, Americans found psychic balm in that Jewish invention: a sense of communal feeling and common destiny. Contemporary scholars of race have discussed Jewish Americanization as a process in which Jews "became white." The song standards are artifacts not just of that Jewish "whitening" but of the way everyone from Israel Baline of Tyumen, Siberia, to Cole Porter of Peru, Indiana, to Harry Lillis Crosby of Spokane, Washington, to Francis Albert Sinatra of Hoboken, New Jersey, remade themselves in the cauldron of American showbiz, and in the process, helped create an enlarged and more democratic idea of what an American was.

Irving Berlin had a great deal at stake in the making of that new-fangled all-Americanism. He knew firsthand the bruising trauma of immigrant life, the sting of the "greenhorn" stigma. He was the sole immigrant among the elite Jewish songwriters of that golden period; Kern, the Gershwins, Rodgers, Hart, Arlen—all were native-born Americans. The historian Jeffrey Melnick has argued that in contrast to the confident cosmopolitanism of Tin Pan Alley Jews such as Gershwin, Berlin's "overt crowd pleasing" bespoke "a certain anxiety about his authority to speak American." To be sure, the Brooklyn-born Gershwin wore his Americanness with greater ease than his friend the Russian immigrant; it is impossible to imagine the urbane composer of "Rhapsody in Blue" producing such unblushingly earnest Americana as "God Bless America" and "White Christmas."

But if Berlin's immigrant anxiety made his music less suave, it compelled him to drive deeper into the bedrock of national myth. With "Alexander's Ragtime Band," Berlin announced a cheerful revolt against the prejudices of Victorian America. Three decades later, pining for a perfect New England Christmas "just like the ones I used to know," he dared to dream himself back into the country's Victorian yesteryear.

6

The Voice of Christmas

"Santa Cros": Bring Crosby in 1954.
Courtesy of Underwood & Underwood/Corbis.

I am not willing to sign any contract before they have
signed Crosby.

—IRVING BERLIN,
to his attorney George Cohen, January 1941

IN THE AUTUMN of 1935, Jack Kapp, the founder and president of Decca Records, approached his star singer, Bing
Crosby, with what seemed to Crosby a preposterous idea.
Kapp, a genial butterball of a man and one of the shrewdest
minds in the record business, had fixed his eye on Christmas
and decided that Crosby should record a pair of holiday carols:
"Adeste Fideles" and "Silent Night." Crosby was under exclusive contract to Decca, and Kapp was his Svengali; a year earlier, Kapp had signed the singer as the franchise voice of his
fledgling label, determined to transform him from a jazz
vocalist with a slightly roguish reputation—his taste for a tip-
ple was well known—into something grander: a "semiclassical
. . . John McCormack of this generation."

At Kapp's urging, Crosby undertook a spectacularly varied
program of recordings. "Jack wouldn't let me get typed,"
Crosby would recall. "I sang hillbillies and blues, ballads and

Victor Herbert, traditional songs and patriotic songs, light opera and even an opera aria or two." Few performers had the chops to move so fluidly from genre to genre, but Crosby was a special singer, who had absorbed the pathos-rich emoting of Al Jolson, the exuberant swing of Louis Armstrong, and a variety of other influences into a singular style that Armstrong likened to "gold being poured out of a cup."

Above all, Crosby's was a modern voice. In the 1920s, technology transformed an entertainment industry known for boisterous expressiveness—the broad jokes and circus antics of vaudeville performers, the mugging and gesticulating of silent movie actors, "coon shouters" bellowing their songs to the variety-show cheap seats—into something more intimate. In motion picture talkies, audiences eavesdropped on lovers' murmured confidences; listening to phonograph records and commercial radio—which beginning in the early 1920s had overtaken sheet music as the song industry's primary means of marketing its product—Americans heard songs delivered in a startlingly different fashion: as gently cooed meditations and confessions. The biggest hit record of the 1920s was a Paul Whiteman Orchestra tune with a revealing title: "Whispering."

Crosby had been listening to recorded music since his Washington boyhood—his family was the first in its neighborhood to have a windup gramophone—and even on his earliest mid-1920s recordings with the Whiteman Orchestra, it was clear that he was in the vanguard of contemporary singers, with an easygoing vocal approach that exploited the power of that magical new tool, the microphone, to create a softer, more records- and radio-friendly sound. For a time, the singer's mild style got him lumped in with a new breed of milquetoast "crooners"—Dick Powell, Gene Austin, Jack Smith, Russ Columbo, the wildly popular Rudy Vallée—but Crosby was a cut above. His muscular baritone and jazzman's sense of swing set him apart from the likes of Vallée, in whose pleading tenor there was a vulnerability that critics derided as effeminate.

Crosby's singing was different: at once robustly masculine and intimate, stately and casual—a style that reconciled, as the critic Will Friedwald has put it, "rhythm with romance." The combination would prove irresistible. More than any other performer, Crosby embodied the Everyman character in whose genial voice Tin Pan Alley's tunesmiths wrote their songs. (Crosby himself ascribed his success to the fact that his fans thought they could sing like him in the shower.) With casually dropped *g*'s and slangy insouciance, Crosby's singing projected modesty, conviviality—qualities he brought to his screen roles in what, by the mid-1930s, was a flourishing Hollywood career. At the same time, the care and intelligence with which he dramatized song lyrics seemed to elevate the Tin Pan Alley pop song to a new artistic level, a feat that not only validated the middle-class experience those songs described, but enshrined it as a kind of romantic ideal.

Eventually Kapp's hopes for the singer would be extravagantly realized. As a hitmaker, Crosby remains unmatched. Three hundred ninety-six of his recordings made the charts, nearly two hundred more than his nearest rival; thirty-eight of those songs hit number one, fully fourteen more than the next closest artist, the Beatles. His total worldwide record sales have topped 400 million.

But Crosby was more than a titan of the Hit Parade. His amiable middle-American persona, amplified in the movies, in jocular asides on his Thursday night *Kraft Music Hall* radio show, and in his hundreds of Decca Records releases, made him biggest multimedia star of the first half of the twentieth century—a pop personality, writ skyscraper-large. As many as 50 million people listened to Crosby's weekly radio broadcasts; in a national poll in the late 1940s, Americans voted Crosby the most admired man alive. He had many nicknames—Der Bingle, the Groaner, Santa Cros—but one was especially telling: Old Dad.

In a 1953 essay, Whitney Baillet offered a crisp summary of Crosby's appeal:

He is handsome, but his ears keep him from being sleek. . . . He is a staunch family man. He is a good athlete. He is no intellectual. He can hold a decent amount of liquor. He is a good guy. He is naïve-seeming. He is, with his pipe, serene, relaxed, unhurrying. He is unassuming. He has a smile that is as warm and broad and white as a feather bed. . . . He has emerged as a figure that is often affectionately regarded as the ideal American male. If, in a larger sense, the bigger-than-life common man is a new figure to the world and is the century's hero, Bing may also be one of the first of the Universal Common Men.

Back in the fall of 1935, that persona was starting to assemble. Whether Crosby was singing jazzy rhythm numbers or cowboy songs or love ballads, listeners were transfixed; the more genres he tackled, the more "universal" his appeal.

Thus Kapp's Christmas gambit. To Kapp's mind, it was the logical next step in Crosby's "semiclassical" transformation. The singer had recently proved his gravitas by singing a pair of turn-of-the-century parlor ballads, "Just a-Wearyin' for You" and "I Love You Truly." Why not venture back into the nineteenth century to record some sacred seasonal favorites? How could the increasingly Crosby-infatuated public resist welcoming the singer into their homes at Christmastime?

Crosby, though, was unconvinced. He was a devout Catholic—he'd attended the Jesuit Gonzaga University and for a time considered the priesthood—and tackling religious music was a daunting step too far: borderline sacrilege. What's more, hymns like "Adeste Fideles" and "Silent Night" were considered too rarefied for pop singers—the domain of "high-class" operatic tenors and church choirs.

But Kapp wouldn't give in. Finally, the two struck a compromise: Crosby would record the songs, but all profits from their sales would be donated to an American Catholic mission in China. On Wednesday, November 13, 1935, Crosby strode into Decca's Hollywood studio and, in just three hours— "one-take Crosby" was famous for his brisk recording sessions—laid down the songs, backed by Georgie Stoll & His Orchestra.

Two weeks later, Decca released a 78 rpm record of "Adeste Fideles" and "Silent Night." Crosby's performances were a touch hesistant—he was still cowed by the material's High Church mystique and tripped over the Latin in "Adeste

Fideles"—but the record was a hit, selling 250,000 copies. As the decade progressed, Crosby and Christmas became linked in the popular imagination. Each year, millions of Americans tuned in to the *Kraft Music Hall* show to hear Crosby singing Christmas hymns in the weeks leading up to the holiday. An evolution was under way: the crooner was becoming "the Voice of Christmas."

Today, when the holiday season brings a flood of Christmas record releases—when carols from "Hark! The Herald Angels Sing" to "Jingle Bells" to "Rudolph the Red-Nosed Reindeer" are among the world's most ubiquitous and best-loved songs—we can scarcely imagine a time when Christmas songs were not a part of the commercial music mainstream. Yet when Crosby's records were released, Christmas music had not yet emerged as a viable pop genre.

Not surprisingly, Irving Berlin—that obsessive seeker of hitmaking "angles"—had tried to kick-start the Tin Pan Alley Christmas song some years before. In 1912, Berlin published "Christmas Time Seems Years and Years Away," a rather pedestrian ballad, whose lyric vaguely foreshadowed the wistful pining in the "White Christmas" chorus. Four years later, Berlin wrote a yuletide rag, "Santa Claus—A Syncopated Christmas Song." Evidently, Berlin didn't care much for the number—it appeared in the Christmas Eve edition of the *New York World,* but he never published its sheet music—and despite a clever rhyme (*chimney/Jim'ny*) in its verse and a couple of nifty chord changes in its chorus, one can't help but think that the songwriter exercised good judgment.

What is noteworthy about Berlin's early Christmas songs

is their novelty. The motley mix of ballads, rags, dance songs, and comic and topical numbers that Tin Pan Alley churned out before World War I touched on seemingly every aspect of American civic life; yet holiday songs were scarce. In music-business trade journals from the period, filled with casual references to dozens of song types—"the German dialect song," "the summer song," "the Aeroplane song"—mentions of Christmas songs are nowhere to be found. For an industry that sought to exploit every minor news event and fleeting public fancy with tailor-made songs, the failure to capitalize on Christmas is, to say the least, surprising. Berlin had glimpsed the commercial potential of Christmas songs, but here his timing was off.

Other sectors of the entertainment industry were also slow to drape their products in Christmas tinsel. Prior to the 1933 debut of Radio City Music Hall's *Christmas Spectacular,* vaudeville and Broadway producers rarely staged holiday-themed shows or revues. Though Christmas settings provided background color for many Hollywood movies—the Christmas Eve reconciliation scene was a favorite trope of melodramas in the silent and early sound eras—there were almost no "Christmas movies" as such. The closest American pop culture had to a holiday entertainment staple was *A Christmas Carol.* Beginning in 1936, huge audiences tuned in to hear Lionel Barrymore voice Scrooge in an annual *Christmas Carol* radio broadcast. Film versions of the Dickens classic date back as early as 1908; M-G-M's 1938 production was a marketing milestone—piggybacking on the success of the Barrymore radio plays, the studio released a record 375 prints of the film "so that as many people as possible could see it during the Christmas season."

If the popularity of *A Christmas Carol* and Crosby's "Adeste Fideles"/"Silent Night" signified Americans' growing appetite for Christmas entertainment, they offered a vision of the holiday that was conspicuously not homegrown. The earliest transcription of "Adeste Fideles" was made circa 1740, by an Englishman, John Francis Wade, a plainchant scribe at the English College in Douai, France. A famous, perhaps unreliable account dates the debut of "Silent Night" to Christmas Eve, 1818, at the parish church in the tiny Lower Austrian town of Oberndorf. But whatever the facts of their provenance, the carols likely struck Crosby's listeners as quintessentially British and Victorian, resonating with the same sentimental Anglophile American imagination that embraced the ghosts, gaslights, and snow-dusted cobblestones of Dickens's yule. To a country that continued to conceive of Christmas as a part of its English heritage, the appeal of these imported icons is understandable. But by the 1930s, the holiday was taking a peculiarly American shape, mingling the gaudy pizzazz of urban commercial culture with soft-focus images of the country's own Victorian past, largely de-Christianized, but retaining a mystical aura as a season of goodwill, merriment, and magic. The entertainment industry had yet to produce holiday fare that reflected a modern, distinctly American Christmas. That task would fall to Irving Berlin.

Throughout his career, Berlin had the good fortune—and the savvy—to hitch his songs' fortunes to the right stars. In the swaggering heyday of vaudeville, Berlin's most important tunes were championed by Jolson, the era's biggest star, capable of just the kind of balcony-rattling bombast songs like "Alexander's Ragtime Band" demanded ("Come on and hear," indeed). In the "swellegant" thirties, Fred Astaire—that singing and dancing Deco objet d'art—was the ideal ambassador for "Cheek to Cheek," "Let's Face the Music and Dance," and other debonair Berlin tunes.

Crosby would be a third great Berlin collaborator—the ideal voice for a new era of musical earnestness. This potent alliance had been a long time coming. Though their paths had crossed several times over the years, this was, Berlin told Jack Kapp, "the first break that I have ever had with Bing Crosby." Crosby had recorded a number of Berlin songs—what singer of that era could have avoided him?—but his choices were oddly peripheral: lesser Berlin numbers such as "Sunshine," "Coquette," "Waiting at the End of the Road," "When the Folks High Up Do the Mean Low Down." The only big Berlin hit that Crosby had cut was "God Bless America."

But for "White Christmas," Crosby was the inevitable choice. Berlin let it be known that he would do the *Holiday Inn* deal with Paramount Pictures only if the studio delivered the singer. In a letter to his attorney George Cohen in January 1941, Berlin was blunt: "I am not willing to sign any contract before they have signed Crosby."

Though Berlin and Crosby were temperamental opposites—the songwriter was a nerve-wracked control freak, Crosby a study in unruffled nonchalance—the pair were professional kindred spirits. Each was the most prolific practitioner of his métier—no one wrote more songs than Berlin or recorded more than Crosby—and though Kapp had to prod Crosby toward the genre-hopping that came naturally to Berlin, the eclecticism of their output bespoke a shared musical open-mindedness. Above all, both men were populists, with an abiding faith in mass taste; and both wore their artfulness so lightly that highbrows and other spoilsports could deny it was even there.

The film that inaugurated the mighty Berlin-Crosby collaboration was a spirited trifle. In his earliest notes for *Holiday Inn,* dated April 17, 1941, Berlin outlined a hackneyed "two boys and a girl setup" whose real purpose, he made clear, was to "use as many holidays as possible." Present in those first notes was an outline of the film's central gimmick—Berlin's own brainchild, of which he was evidently proud (he insisted on being credited with the film's "original idea" in its opening titles):

> The character, Bing Crosby, around whom this idea motivates, is very much like Bing Crosby without Crosby's ambition. When he saved enough money he bought a farm, and finding it tough going he hit upon the idea of turning the farm into an Inn that would be open only on holidays.

Berlin spent the rest of April at the Arrowhead Springs Resort in San Bernardino, California, with Mark Sandrich and Paramount executive Gene Meyers, refining the movie's rather dopey plot, which, as in so many Berlin films, was a "backstager," set in the showbiz milieu the songwriter knew best. Crosby's character, Jim Hardy, is one-half of a successful song-and-dance team who, tired of his grueling performing schedule and frenetic city life, decides to retire to a Connecticut farm with his fiancée. On the eve of his retirement, he gets some bad news: the hoofer Ted Hanover, his rakish partner, has taken up with Jim's girl. So Jim makes his rustic retreat alone.

After a lonely year on the farm, Jim decides to return to the show business game, but in a novel way: he converts his farmhouse to an inn, open to the public on holidays only, complete with lavish holiday-themed floor shows. With this absurd plot contrivance—suddenly Jim's New England cottage is roomy enough to accommodate hundreds of guests, a full orchestra, and a Vegas-sized phalanx of dancing girls—arrives a steady flow of Berlin's holiday songs and a love interest: Linda Mason, a pretty, good-hearted singer and dancer, hired by Jim to work at the inn. The two quickly strike up a romance.

All is going well until Ted, Jim's erstwhile partner, arrives with a movie producer, discovers Linda, and whisks her away to Hollywood to star in a film based on Jim's inn. Jim mopes around for a while, then pulls himself together; he flies out to Hollywood to win Linda back; and the story comes to a predictable, happy, tuneful conclusion.

It would take eight months, two scenarists, and several screenplay revisions until the particulars of that story were nailed down. (In one draft, the leading lady is introduced in a flashback as a hard-luck child of the Lower East Side; in another, she is a socialite.) What is noteworthy about the various versions of the plot is the prominence of "White Christmas." From the beginning, Berlin intended that the song be the film's centerpiece and linchpin of its love story. Where the movie's other songs are elaborate production numbers, "White Christmas" stands out in its homely simplicity: it appears twice in *Holiday Inn*, staged both times as a tender ballad sung at a piano.

In September 1941, nearly two years after he had brought "White Christmas" into his office, Irving Berlin arrived in Los Angeles to begin production on *Holiday Inn*. Berlin and Sandrich had managed, after much wrangling with Paramount executives, to assemble a dream duo of leading men: alongside Crosby, the nation's biggest singing star, they had hired its top dancer, Fred Astaire. The cost of those two stars forced the studio to seek a cut-rate leading lady, so instead of Berlin's first choice, Mary Martin, the part of Linda Mason went to a newcomer, Marjorie Reynolds, a bland blonde who couldn't sing. (In the famous scenes where she joins Crosby in singing "White Christmas," Reynolds is lip-synching Martha Mears's vocal track.)

Berlin had spent much of the previous summer in New York working on songs for the film, testing them out on everyone from Helmy Kresa to Elmer Rice, the Federal Theater playwright who had contracted with Paramount to help out with the *Holiday Inn* script. The result of the songwriter's labors was his largest-ever film score: eleven new Berlin songs, accompanied in the film by two chestnuts, "Lazy" and the inevitable "Easter Parade."

The score wasn't quite the equal-opportunity panorama of

American holidays—a song for Christmas, a song for Passover, a Chinese New Year number—that Berlin had once envisioned; nor was it full of impish songs that "debunked the holiday spirit." It was, overall, a somewhat stolid effort: a collection of earnest, tuneful, and pleasant songs, not nearly as inspired as those he had composed for *Top Hat*—and would again, a few years hence, for the Broadway hit *Annie Get Your Gun*. Songs like "I Can't Tell a Lie," a Washington's birthday number, and "Let's Start the New Year Right" were transparently throwaway; "You're Easy to Dance With" and "Be Careful, It's My Heart" were fine, lilting love ballads but didn't rise to the level of Berlin's standard-setting work in that genre. *Holiday Inn*'s more ambitious songs also fell short. "Song of Freedom," a blast of Fourth of July patriotism that Crosby sings in front of flickering newsreel footage of American warships, was an awkward attempt at a kind of stentorian swing— the Miller band does "God Bless America."

In fact, *Holiday Inn*'s score had only one great song, and Berlin knew it. From the first day that he arrived at Paramount Studios on Melrose Boulevard to begin work on the picture, the songwriter was obsessed with "White Christmas." The man who faced the brunt of Berlin's anxieties was Walter Scharf, the Paramount staff arranger charged with turning Berlin's tunes into full-fledged orchestrations.

That difficult work would take place over a few weeks in Scharf's small office in the music building on the Paramount lot. There, on a transposing piano—another Berlin "Buick"— the songwriter first ran through the score for Scharf, Sandrich, and a battery of studio executives. Scharf remembered Berlin's performance of his new Christmas number: a halting, "very rough" rendition that left the assembled listeners scratching their heads. "It was almost like a child playing with three fingers," Scharf recalled. "Nobody knew what to make of it."

Bing Crosby's first reaction to "White Christmas" was equally befuddled. Berlin, who confessed to being "nervous as a rabbit sniffing stew" when demonstrating the song for Crosby in his Paramount dressing room, was cheered by the singer's reaction. "Irving," said Crosby, "you won't have to worry about that one." But privately, Crosby wasn't so sanguine. When Scharf told the singer that he thought "White Christmas" would turn out well, Crosby rolled his eyes: "I *hope* so."

Scharf was faced with the tricky task that had confronted Helmy Kresa and Berlin's other musical secretaries: translating into music the sounds that Berlin heard in his exacting inner ear but lacked the technical vocabulary to communicate. This work called for an unusual kind of collaboration, which seemed to invert the natural artistic hierarchy, putting Berlin at the mercy of lesser creators. But in the case of "White Christmas," as Scharf quickly learned, it was hardly a true collaboration at all: Berlin was in charge. "He knew exactly what he wanted," Scharf recalled, "It was just tough for him to explain because he had no musical training."

Scharf began by "scratching out a lead sheet in another key," giving Berlin's melody a "harmony part that had a finish to it." After hearing the songwriter run through the tune in his stammering fashion several more times, Scharf had begun to understand Berlin's "intuition it would be a special song." The orchestrator heard a folklike starkness in "White Christmas" and proposed an austere, brazenly un-Hollywood arrangement, featuring a sole acoustic guitar and an upright bass. It is a pity that Berlin dismissed the suggestion; how many treacle-smothered versions might the world have been spared had the song first appeared as a finger-picked pastorale? Although Berlin was a lifelong champion of musical simplicity, he was firm that "White Christmas" be given the "class" treatment worthy of a big-movie musical ballad, and so he and Scharf set about creating a full-orchestra arrangement.

This was accomplished through a process of musical trial and error. Berlin hummeed the music he heard in his head; Scharf attempted to replicate those sounds, noodling on the piano until he hit upon just the right chord or series of notes. For Berlin, the painstaking work on "White Christmas" was, Scharf remembered, "a tremendously traumatic experience. . . . It was as if he were going to have a baby when he was working on that song." Even when the songwriter was no longer needed—when Scharf was making final transcriptions of the orchestrations that the pair had decided upon—Berlin couldn't tear himself away from the work. Rather than go back to his hotel, the songwriter camped out in Scharf's office, catching the odd hour of sleep on the sofa while Scharf toiled at the nearby piano.

The result was an orchestration of impressive subtlety and lightness: a delicate swirl of vibrato-rich violins and trilling woodwinds that served mostly as gentle accompaniment to the vocal. To Berlin's delight, his lyrics and main melody line were thrust right out front.

With the "White Christmas" arrangement in place, Berlin

now had the recording of the song to fret over. On the after-noon of that recording—the "prerecording" of the track that Crosby would lip-synch in the film—Berlin was frenzied. "I'd never seen a man so wrapped up in himself," Scharf recalled. Thinking it wise to get the songwriter out of their hair, Scharf and Sandrich urged him to go back to his hotel to get some rest. "We probably won't get around to doing the tracks for hours," Scharf told Berlin.

The session was speedy: Crosby stepped to the microphone and finished "White Christmas" in his usual two takes. Imme-diately following the successful second pass, Scharf marched over to the far corner of the Studio 5 soundstage: he had noticed a couple of large soundproofing flats heaped higgledy-piggledy in a corner and was worried that they would interfere with the ambience of the recordings. When he looked behind the flats, he beheld a preposterous sight: the crouched figure of Irving Berlin, staring sheepishly up at him. "I'm sorry," Berlin said. "I couldn't bring myself to go. . . . So when are you going to start the recording?" The songwriter thought that the performance he had been listening to was a rehearsal. But the song was done: Crosby had already left to play a round of golf.

When the prerecording of the *Holiday Inn* score was com-plete, Berlin's job was done; Sandrich and company could be forgiven a sigh of sweet relief when the songwriter packed up his neuroses and headed back to New York in time for Christ-mas, 1941. After the New Year, the actual film shoot got under way; with Sandrich's assured hand at the helm, it proceeded smoothly and without event. There was some minor tension on the set between the film's costars. Crosby's carefree, two-

piano at the inn. The song is reprised in the film's denoue-
ment, on the film-set replica of the inn, where fake snow falls
from soundstage rafters and Linda has realized that her success is not as fulfilling as the love she left behind in Connecticut. In *Holiday Inn*, Astaire's urban sharpie is defeated by
Crosby and "White Christmas"; in the real world of pop culture, Crosby and "White Christmas" would put an exclama-
tion point on the end of the glitzy era that Astaire embodied.

Holiday Inn is so obviously featherweight that it might seem
absurd to plumb the film for deeper meaning. But its home-
coming theme—Jim Hardy's withdrawal from big-city hulla-
baloo to the haven of his farmhouse inn; Linda Mason's happy
return to the same farmhouse after her empty Hollywood success—reveals more about the musical heritage of "White
Christmas." For although "White Christmas" is ostensibly a
Christmas tune, deeper connections link it to another song
genre, one of the oldest and most durable in American music:
home songs, ballads of yearning for lost rustic abodes. The
genre's lineage stretches back to the parlor songs of the antebellum nineteenth century, when the favorite themes of childhood innocence, motherly love, and doomed nostalgia were
expressed in odes to the pastoral home ("Home! Sweet
Home!" "The Cottage of My Mother," "O Give Me a Home by
the Sea"). The home-song theme stirs in Thomas Moore's Irish
songs of the 1840s and 50s ("Erin, the Tear and the Smile in
Thine Eyes"), in mid-nineteenth-century German-American
folk songs ("When the Swallows Homeward Fly"), and, most
famously, in the "old home" fantasies of Stephen Foster ("The
Old Folks at Home," "My Old Kentucky Home"). In pre–World

War I Tin Pan Alley, the craze for ethnic caricature gave the home song new life, as vaudeville comedians sang laments in the homesick voices of Irish, Jewish, Italian, German, Greek, and Chinese immigrants. And home songs endured through the twentieth century, resurfacing in the nostalgic plaints of country balladeers and Chicago bluesmen, and in soul standards like Gladys Knight and the Pips's "Midnight Train to Georgia," the story of a southerner fleeing Los Angeles with a "one-way ticket . . . back to a simpler place and time."

We can recognize why this genre would exert a powerful pull on Americans' imaginations. The United States is a place of rootlessness and nomadism, and homesickness might be called the American affliction: a condition intrinsic to a nation of immigrants, slaves, and vanquished natives. For almost two hundred years, the home song has spoken to newly arrived citizens from overseas, to migrants moving west, to country folk transplanted to cities. Time and again, Americans' desire for stability and safety has been expressed in paeans to a bucolic abode—a cottage by the sea, a home on the range, a dream of good old days way down upon the Swanee River, far, far away.

Berlin's elegiac "White Christmas" lyric ties the song explicitly to the home song tradition. All the conventions of the genre are here: the dream of a rustic idyll that is temporally and geographically remote, images of pastoral serenity, the association of happy times in distant days with childhood innocence and wonder. Berlin idolized Stephen Foster—for years, a portrait of the composer hung on his office wall—and the spirit of that greatest of all home song specialists lurks in "White Christmas." Compare Berlin's "May your days be

merry and bright" with a couplet from "My Old Kentucky
Home": "The young folks roll on the little cabin floor / All
merry, all happy and bright."

The place of "White Christmas" in the home song tradition sheds more light on its origins as novelty number: Berlin's
tune looks suspiciously like a home-song spoof. His Beverly
Hills sophisticate who yearns for snowy northern climes is a
mirror-image inversion of a standard home song character,
found in literally hundreds of Tin Pan Alley songs of the first
part of the century: the homely—usually black—Dixieland
exile, stranded in the chilly north, far from his sultry home
turf. Indeed, from postbellum minstrel show songs to turn-of-
the-century Tin Pan Alley "coon songs," the most persistent
home-song trope was that of a black man mooning over the
memory of his Southern home—a freed slave, longing to
return to the plantation. Consider the most famous home
song of them all, Foster's "The Old Folks at Home":

> All up and down de whole creation,
> Sadly I roam,
> Still longing for de old plantation,
> And for the old folks at home . . .
> Oh! darkeys how my heart grows weary,
> Far from de old folks at home.

Blackface minstrelsy is, of course, a tradition that haunts
American music from Foster to Eminem; a scholarly lifetime
could be spent trying to parse the mixture of fear, loathing,
and desire that surrounded a blackface performance of lyrics

like those in Gus Adams's "My Home on Old Virginny Shore": "I'd sooner be a slave for poor old Massah who now in his grave / Den in de richest places to dwell." That song was published in 1881, the year that the great Eastern European Jewish exodus began, and from the moment that Jews first set foot on variety-show stages and in song-publishing offices, they took to the all-American art of blackface minstrelsy with special zeal. The most famous Jewish minstrel was Al Jolson, who donned burnt cork to graduate from immigrant cantor's son to American "jazz singer," but the tradition is long, reaching from Jolson to Eddie Cantor to Mezz Mezzrow to the Beastie Boys. In turn-of-the-century Tin Pan Alley the blackface home song was something of a Jewish specialty; notably, both Irving Berlin's and George Gershwin's break-through hits ("Alexander's Ragtime Band" and "Swanee," respectively) featured musical allusions to "The Old Folks at Home."

In his early career, Berlin tried his hand at nearly every song type, but he had a special affinity for blackface numbers and home songs. Between 1912 and 1925 he wrote at least twenty home songs, the majority of them blackface "Dixie" numbers; one of his biggest early hits was "When the Midnight Choo-Choo Leaves for Alabam'," published in 1912— sixty-one years before Gladys Knight's "Midnight Train" song hit number one on the *Billboard* charts. During his ragtime king period, Berlin was so closely associated with blackface music that he was dogged by rumors that a "colored boy" was ghostwriting his tunes, an accusation he joked about in a poem he sent to songwriter Harry Ruby in 1970:

Of all the Tin Pan Alley Greats
Berlin is the tops.
A "colored boy" writes all his hits—
But who writes all his flops?

The minstrelsy tradition is invoked in a surprisingly explicit manner in *Holiday Inn*. If Berlin's Christmas song "whitens" plantation nostalgia, transplanting the longed-for home from sultry Dixie to snowy New England, *Holiday Inn* blacks "White Christmas" up all over again, turning Jim Hardy's "Midville, Connecticut," farmhouse into a kind of Tara North. The first hint of plantation overtones comes some thirty minutes into the film, when we meet Jim's live-in help: his maid, Mamie, and her two children Daphne and Vanderbilt. This threesome embodies a breathtaking medley of Hollywood's most infamous racist stereotypes. Mamie is an obese, kerchiefed Aunt Jemima, played by Louise Beavers in a note-perfect rendition of the stock type—a type enshrined by Hollywood just two years earlier when Hattie McDaniel won the Academy Award for her portrayal of Scarlet O'Hara's maid in *Gone With the Wind*. Mamie's role in *Holiday Inn*'s drama is telegraphed by her name, just a vowel-sound away from "Mammy." She has no man in her life—no life of her own— and exists primarily to mother Jim and Linda; "I knows Miss Linda better than I knows my own kids," she tells Jim. As for her own children: they function as "comic relief." A tangle of nappy braids sprouts atop bug-eyed Daphne's little head. Vanderbilt's name invokes the minstrelsy convention of giving black males comically high-class names: Vanderbilt shares his name with a billionaire, but his real "darky" character is revealed when the camera lingers on him in the kitchen, chomping on a chicken wing twice the size of his face.

In and of themselves, these images aren't especially revealing—mere reminders of how recently this sort of caricature was considered an amusing cinematic divertissement. But the relentlessness of the blackface imagery in *Holiday Inn* suggests there is more here: Berlin's film calls attention to the peculiar pedigree of its centerpiece song.

The most overt moment of minstrelsy comes in the middle of the film, when Jim and Linda perform Berlin's Lincoln's birthday number, "Abraham," in blackface. Crosby, dressed as a black Lincoln, delivers the song in a shucking-and-jiving dialect, as a swinging spiritual filled with lusty "Negroid" asides ("Yeah, man!"). But the more telling scene is one just prior to the "Abraham" performance. Jim has insisted that he and Linda black up: he wants to hide his girl from Ted Hanover, the rogue who has designs on stealing her away from Jim and the inn. While painting Linda's face in a backstage dressing room, Jim proposes marriage. Here, the film's key themes—its love story and its vision of a happy country home as a bulwark against modernity and shallow big-city values—converge around the wearing of blackface. Behind the black mask, Linda is invisible to Ted Hanover, Jim and Linda's romance is safe, the nostalgic dream of their life at the inn is preserved. What song plays in the background while Jim proposes marriage and tenderly spreads burnt cork on his beloved's face? A lulling instrumental version of Berlin's holiday home song, "White Christmas."

The point, of course, is not that Berlin was racist, or that "White Christmas" is a racist song. Indeed, in many ways Berlin distinguished himself from prevailing racial attitudes. Six years before Billie Holiday introduced "Strange Fruit," Berlin's "Supper Time" was the first pop song to treat the national shame of lynching. The troupe with which Berlin toured the world performing his World War II revue *This Is the Army* was the Army's first integrated unit; the performers lived and traveled together, and Berlin refused invitations to social engagements unless the entire cast was invited.

Whether or not Berlin was conscious of the undertones in *Holiday Inn* is an open question. But one can't help reading the blackface imagery in *Holiday Inn* as the shadow history of "White Christmas" returning to haunt the song—once again, primordial American homesickness is overlapping with American racial obsession. In the home song tradition we find a variation on the "outrageous" sentimental dream that Leslie Fielder identified in *The Adventures of Huckleberry Finn* and *Moby-Dick,* where white social outcasts, forlorn and forsaken, seek solace in the arms of a black man. The musical case is slightly different from the literary one: the hapless home song dreamer wants not to be embraced by the black man but to become him. When white musicians go for broke, when they try to wring the most pathos from their songs, to express the deepest sort of American desolation, they invariably beat a retreat to minstrelsy; think of Van Morrison or Mick Jagger or any of countless other white rock performers, dropping into a southern-tinged "black" accent, as if channeling the grief-hounded spirit of a sharecropper. That rich, fraught musical tradition simmers beneath the surface of America's most beloved sentimental ballad. Certainly, Berlin understood the heritage on which his yuletide home song drew. "Let me sing of Dixie's charms / Of cotton fields and Mammy's arms," he wrote in 1928. "And if my song can make you homesick, / I'm happy."

Berlin returned to New York in late December of 1941, his work on *Holiday Inn* finished. (The actual shoot and postproduction would continue in Hollywood for several months.) What the songwriter scarcely realized was that the most significant development in the saga of "White Christmas" was to take place some months later, in the spring of 1942, back in California. At eight-thirty on the morning of May 29, Bing Crosby entered Decca Studios in Los Angeles to record several songs from *Holiday Inn* for a collection of 78s to be released in conjunction with the film. Among the songs he recorded that morning was "White Christmas." Backed by the John Trotter Orchestra and the Ken Darby singers, Crosby cut the song with his usual cool dispatch, requiring two takes and eighteen minutes of studio time. He would have needed only a single take were it not for a fatal flub—he swallowed the *your* in "may all your Christmases"—in the song's third-to-last bar.

Berlin knew that the Crosby session was taking place but didn't pay it much mind—he was preoccupied with other projects. In an April letter, he had urged Jack Kapp to "keep these songs simple. . . . This is one score, especially the ballads, that should not be over-arranged." In late July, Berlin heard the records, told Kapp rather perfunctorily that he was "thrilled" with them, and left it at that.

As engaged as Berlin was with the business side of his songwriting enterprise—for all his obsessive vigilance about all aspects of his songs' promotion—he hadn't fully grasped the importance of records in making song hits. He was conditioned by a lifetime of Tin Pan Alley experience to focus on sheet music sales and the show—or in this case, the movie. The record business was still, in relative terms, a fledgling industry; and though he earned royalties from recordings of his songs, records didn't butter Berlin's bread.

Crosby's "White Christmas" record would change all that. Although Kapp had a reputation for laying it on thick in the studio—Astaire warned Berlin that Decca's records were "mediocre stuff"—he heeded Berlin's plea for simplicity. The song is given a delicate orchestral arrangement, enveloping Crosby's baritone in a feather bed of strings and tolling chimes; Berlin had to be pleased to hear his song treated with the same care as "Silent Night" and "Adeste Fideles." Even the appearance of the Ken Darby singers, who reprise the chorus after Crosby's first run-through, doesn't break the record's gentle spell.

"A jackdaw with a cleft palate could have sung it successfully," Crosby once said of "White Christmas." "You've got to give full credit to its composer, Irving Berlin." But countless lesser "White Christmas" recordings tell a different story. Crosby was a master at pitching his performance to suit a song's emotional requirements. Listening to his greatest recordings, we hear one perfectly realized mood piece after another, from the sumptuous romanticism of "Where the Blue of the Night (Meets the Gold of the Day)" to the swatting-flies-on-the-front-porch breeziness of his "Gone Fishin'" duet with Louis Armstrong to the jaundiced rumination of "I'm Thru with Love." No one else has summoned quite the same combination of reverence and restraint that "White Christmas" requires.

Crosby enunciates Berlin's lyric with stately care, treating "White Christmas" like a carol—a meaningful choice given the novelty of secular Christmas songs in 1942. But "White Christmas" also sounds like a love song. In the tune's second measure, on the first syllable of the word *dreaming,* Crosby lets fly a telltale mordent—a mournful fluttering from F to G and back again—a Crosby signature that stamps "White Christmas" as a pop song in the sentimental crooner tradition. (He repeats the trick on the first syllable of *sleighbells* in bar fourteen.) No less an authority than Berlin's eldest daughter, Mary Ellin Barrett, a teenager at the time of the song's release, remembers how Crosby's performance gave "White Christmas" an erotic charge. "However seasonal the words, we didn't hear it as a carol," she recalled. " 'White Christmas' [was] a song boys and girls . . . danced to, fell in love to, adopted as 'their' song . . . a ballad that Bing Crosby had sung to a blonde in a movie."

But the heart of "White Christmas" is its creeping melancholy. This Crosby captures wonderfully, with many small touches: with the sob that surfaces in "*dream*ing," with the soul cry he brings to the song's key line "just like the ones I used to know." There is spookiness in Berlin's lyric—the narrator is that ghostly figure, gazing dimly back at the past—and we hear that quality in Crosby's voice, never more clearly than in the song's closing moments. Crosby sings a sweet high harmony part, soaring in barbershop falsetto above the female choir ("May your days be merry and bright"); then the background singers fall silent, and Crosby plunges into his burring lower register, dropping a note below the octave in the final phrase—"Christ*mases* *be* white"—before Berlin's melody climbs back to make a valedictory cadence, still trailing the shadow of that eerie almost-dissonance.

7

A War Tonic

✦

"Dreaming of a white Christmas":
American G.I.s trim a holiday tree in a captured German town.
Courtesy of Bettmann/Corbis.

What have we learned? Flame and death out of the sky over Pearl Harbor one year since—and have there been lessons? . . . We have learned to be a little sad and a little lonesome, without being sickly about it. This feeling is caught in the song of a thousand juke boxes and the tune whistled in streets and homes, "I'm Dreaming of a White Christmas." When we sing that we don't hate anybody. And there are things that we love that we're going to have sometime soon if the breaks are not too bad against us. "May all your days be merry and bright—and may all your Christmases be white." Away down under, this latest hit of Irving Berlin catches us where we love peace . . .

—CARL SANDBURG,
December 6, 1942

My new furnishings were all war surplus. . . . Even my library was largely war surplus, coming as it did from recreation kits intended for troops overseas. . . . And, since phonograph records came in these unused kits, too, I got myself a war-surplus, weather-proofed, portable phonograph, guaranteed to play in any climate from the Bering Straits to the Arafura Sea. By buying the recreation kits, each one a sealed pig-in-a-poke, I came into possession of twenty-six recordings of Bing Crosby's "White Christmas."

—KURT VONNEGUT,
Mother Night

What is a war song?
No less, no more,
Than a song that's popular
During a war.

—IRVING BERLIN,
"What Is a War Song?"

WHEN JAPANESE fighter pilots swept over Pearl Harbor on December 7, 1941, Irving Berlin was in Beverly Hills, enjoying a day off from work on *Holiday Inn* with Ellin, who had traveled west to join her husband. (The "White Christmas" prerecording—the one Berlin eavesdropped on from behind those soundproofing partitions—had likely taken place sometime the preceding week.) The war had been on Berlin's mind for some time. In the years leading up to Pearl Harbor, while the Germans marched inexorably across Europe and North Africa and rained bombs on London, Americans were consumed by an increasingly bitter debate over U.S. engagement in the conflict. Berlin was a strong backer of President Roosevelt in the 1940 election—both he and Ellin spoke at pro-Roosevelt rallies—and was vocal in his support of the president's efforts on behalf of the British. The composer's membership in the Committee to Defend America by Aiding the Allies put him firmly in the interventionist camp.

Of course, Berlin had already tipped his hand. "God Bless America" was inspired by his trip to embattled Britain, and though Berlin called it a "peace song," it was, in its mood of prayerful resolve, unambiguously an interventionist anthem. By the turn of the New Year in 1941, Berlin was writing songs whose politics were more explicit. On February 1, 1941, two topical Berlin songs debuted on the radio broadcast *ASCAP on Parade*: a mournful portrait of bomb-strafed London, "A Little Old Church in England," and "When That Man Is Dead and Gone"—a "timely spiritual," according to its composer, with lyrics forecasting the demise of a certain "Satan with a small mustache." "Incidentally, every picture I have ever seen of the devil had a mustache," Berlin told the *New York Times*.

Those songs were just the first in a string of war-themed Berlin numbers that appeared in the ensuing months. There was "Any Bonds Today?," Berlin's song promoting the defense-bond and saving-stamp drive; "Arms for the Love of America," introduced June 10, in a live broadcast on both NBC and CBS radio, from the steps of the U.S. Capitol; "Angels of Mercy," recorded by Bing Crosby; "I Paid My Income Tax Today," a big hit for Eddie Cantor. The most poignant of the lot was "When This Crazy World Is Sane Again," a plaint in which Berlin included a sly plug for one of his old hits:

When this crazy world is sane again,
When the world starts mending its ways,
We'll go strolling down the lane again
As we did in happier days.
The heavens are cloudy, but storms don't last;
The present and future will soon be the past.
When this crazy world is sane again,
We will all wake up and say,
"Isn't this a lovely day?"

Amid the flurry of topical songs, the public could be forgiven for barely registering the debut of another Berlin tune, on Bing Crosby's Christmas Eve, 1941, *Kraft Music Hall* broadcast, just seventeen days after the Pearl Harbor attack. The show's penultimate number was a sneak preview of an unusual seasonal tune. No tape survives of that history-making broadcast, in which Crosby gave the first public performance of "White Christmas."

Berlin would have to wait another nine months for the public to discover that song, but those months would prove momentous. With his recent tunes, Berlin had staked new claim to the cheerleading mantle he had seized during World War I. The duty-calls largesse of Berlin the Citizen did not always bring out the best in Berlin the Artist. In writing patriotic songs, his taste for the purplish often went unchecked; the hand-on-heart sentiments and forward-march thud of Berlin's wartime anthems have not aged well. But in the immediate aftermath of Pearl Harbor, with the country freshly embarked on a perilous national adventure, Berlin was zealous about his morale-boosting role. "Songs make history," he told the *New York Times*. "And history makes songs."

There was no chance that the fifty-three-year-old Berlin would be drafted into service as he had been in the First World War; this time, he volunteered. He decided to revive and update *Yip Yip Yaphank*: create a new all-soldier revue for the new war, to raise funds for the armed services. In late February of 1942, the songwriter pitched the idea; on March 11, he received a formal letter from the War Department in Washington asking him to undertake the project. "I am delighted to accede to your request," Berlin replied in the elevated diction that he used when corresponding with public officials. "I need not assure you that I will give this all my time because nothing could be closer to my heart."

Berlin immediately set to writing songs and sketches. By late April, the songwriter was back in Camp Upton, the Yaphank, Long Island, base where he had been stationed in 1917, playing drill sergeant to a cast of performers recruited from army camps all over the country. The show was to be called *This Is the Army*; all of its proceeds would benefit the Army Emergency Relief Fund. It would dominate the next four years of Berlin's life. The songwriter took the production to Broadway, then to other major American cities; he filmed a movie version in the spring of 1943, before embarking on a two-and-a-half-year-long international tour, performing for American and British soldiers overseas—sometimes perilously close to battle lines. By the time of the final *This Is the Army* performance in Hawaii in October 1945, Berlin and his troupe had entertained hundreds of thousands of soldiers, in six theaters of operation; they had performed in locations as far-flung as Egypt, Iran, and New Guinea; they had played for the queen in a glittering London theater and for battle-hardened GIs in the Philippines on a rickety makeshift stage fashioned from coconut logs and palm fronds.

The show was a throwback: years after Berlin had begun planning a return to old-fashioned revues, he was finally bringing one to the stage. *This Is the Army* clung closely to the conventions of the genre. It opened with a minstrel show number; there were interludes featuring tumblers and jugglers; there were moments of high camp—brawny soldiers cavorting and kicking in drag—and celebrity impersonations. Above all, there were songs: patriotic tunes, lampoons of the Germans and Japanese, sentimental songs, love ballads, and a slew of songs depicting, with impish good humor, the lot of the everyday enlistee—"This Is the Army, Mister Jones," "My Sergeant and I Are Buddies," "The Army's Made a Man out of Me."

But *This Is the Army*'s most popular tune was its oldest: an interpolation of "Oh! How I Hate to Get Up in the Morning," one of the big hits of World War I, composed in 1918 by a bleary-eyed "Sergeant Irving Berlin." The show's second-to-last number found the songwriter himself at center stage, rising sleepily from his cot in his old World War I doughboy uniform. Over the four years of *This Is the Army*'s run, this number never failed to stop the show; when *This Is the Army* premiered, at the Broadway Theatre in New York, on July 4, 1942, Berlin was greeted by a thunderous standing ovation. Only after a full ten minutes did the Broadway Theatre audience retake its seats and hear Berlin rasp, "Oh! How I hate to get up in the morning! / Oh! How I'd love to remain in bed!"

Exactly one month after *This Is the Army*'s debut, New York played host to another Irving Berlin opening: the gala premiere of *Holiday Inn* at the Paramount Theater. The movie's big draw might have been its milestone pairing of Crosby and Astaire; but the sign on the Paramount marquee—"IRVING BERLIN'S *Holiday Inn*"—left little doubt about the identity of the film's true star. In the flush of *This Is the Army*'s triumph, Berlin had graduated to a new level of celebrity—he was the adored songwriting superpatriot of a nation at war. Even the fluffy *Holiday Inn* was regarded as another gift from Berlin to a needy nation. ("14 songs by Irving Berlin and eight dances by Fred Astaire" exclaimed Paramount Pictures' promotional literature. "It's a war tonic—and it works.") "We know you haven't had much time to think of yourself this past year," radio host Phil Spitalny gushed in a tribute to Berlin on GE's popular Sunday night *Hour of Charm* broadcast. "But America has been thinking about you constantly, singing your songs, and storing them in her heart."

Berlin had become a fund-raising machine, donating the earnings from song after song to patriotic causes. Proceeds from "Angels of Mercy" went to the Red Cross. The royalties from "Any Bonds Today?" and "I Paid My Income Tax Today" benefited the U.S. Treasury Department, and "Arms for the Love of America," the Army Ordnance Department. "God Bless America" had earned untold thousands of dollars for the Boy and Girl Scouts of America; some newspaper reports were speculating that *This Is the Army* might make a million dollars for the Army Emergency Relief Fund. (By the time the show's national tour ended the following February, its earnings would more than double that estimate.) The *Holiday Inn* premiere was a benefit for Navy Relief. "At his present pace, Berlin may soon be worn out from saluting the Army, Navy, Marines and other branches of the service," Irving Hoffman wrote in the *New York Times*. "But so far the critics are not worn out from saluting him."

A particularly grand salute to Berlin preceded the *Holiday Inn* screening at the Paramount: a thirty-minute stage show celebrating the "thirty-fifth anniversary of Irving Berlin in show business." Broadcast live on NBC Radio, the tribute featured a host of all-stars performing Berlin tunes: the Skinnay Ennis Orchestra, the Ink Spots, the Knight Sisters, Willie Shore, Clayton Case, and Al Hendrickson. Berlin himself made a brief appearance on the Paramount stage before racing out the side door, jumping on his bicycle—even for a national hero, the quickest way to negotiate Midtown traffic—and pedaling ten blocks north to the Broadway Theatre, where he threw on his costume in time for his *This Is the Army* star turn. While Berlin belted out "Oh! How I Hate to Get Up in the Morning!" at the corner of Fifty-third and Broadway, a packed house in Times Square watched Bing Crosby sing the songwriter's lilting new ballad about Christmas cards and snowy treetops.

Berlin left the Broadway Theatre that night eagerly anticipating *Holiday Inn*'s overnight reviews. He had every reason to be confident in the film's success. It had been screened for radio executives and orchestra leaders in June, and the reaction had been uniformly enthusiastic. Hollywood bigwigs had endorsed the picture; even Berlin's old friend Samuel Gold-wyn, the head of Paramount's rival studio M-G-M, had raved. Ellin Berlin assured her husband that the audience at the Paramount premiere had left the theater all smiles. By the next morning, Berlin was able to wire Mark Sandrich in Holly-wood reporting notices "unanimous in their praise."

But reading those reviews, Berlin might have felt a pang of disappointment. Though his score was roundly hailed, scarcely a single reviewer had noted "White Christmas," the film's emo-tional centerpiece, the only number that was sung twice and, to Berlin's mind, the highlight of the score. The *Times* referred to "White Christmas" in passing as "tender"; the *Herald Tribune* called it "tuneful"; *Variety* didn't mention the song at all.

The tepid critical response to "White Christmas" seemed to confirm murmurings that had been heard over the last sev-eral months in the Berlin camp. For some time, the songwriter had vied with members of his inner circle—the *Variety* writer Tom Pryor, his lawyer Lewis Gilbert—who claimed that "White Christmas" was too schmaltzy and would be a flop. Perhaps, Berlin brooded, the naysayers had been right. Would "the best song anybody ever wrote" be an also-ran?

For all the accolades he was garnering for *This Is the Army*, Berlin was anxious to make the *Holiday Inn* score "an old-fashioned smash"—a hit to benefit an old-fashioned cause, the Irving Berlin Music Company. To this end, Berlin's plug-ging staff embarked on promotion of the *Holiday Inn* score, determined to make it "the greatest exploitation campaign, in connection with any musical, so far made." Berlin relished the promotional aspects of hitmaking almost as much as he did actual songwriting. "Izzy is uptown, but he's still there with the old downtown hard sell," George M. Cohan had once said of Berlin, and it was true: no matter how "uptown" he became, Berlin kept his lust for arm-twisting and angle-playing in the Tin Pan Alley trenches. When his friend the writer Abel Green, the editor of *Variety*, asked Berlin in 1954 why he was bothering to personally telephone disc jockeys to promote his latest efforts, the songwriter confessed, "I am as much of a song plugger today as I was in 1907 when I was the only one who sang 'Marie from Sunny Italy.'"

With Christmas still months off, Berlin chose to inaugurate the *Holiday Inn* campaign with the movie's Valentine's Day tune, "Be Careful, It's My Heart." Next to "White Christmas," "Be Careful" was a conventional ballad, but it had its moments—some wry lyrical flourishes ("It's not my watch you're holding, it's my heart") and a soulful octave leap in its twenty-third bar—and Crosby's performances, both in the film and on his Decca recording, were typically subtle and stylish. By the time of the *Holiday Inn* premiere, Berlin's plugging campaign—for two months, his staff had stroked, cajoled, threatened, and charmed bandleaders, radio executives, and sheet music jobbers—had paid off: "Be Careful, It's My Heart" had entered the Lucky Strike Hit Parade.

The song would climb as high as number two on that chart, but it stalled there; it was no smash. "You can't high-pressure the great majority of Americans into buying something they don't want," Berlin had once told his lawyer George Cohen. Song publishers, he said, frequently dropped "a lot of money exploiting a song the public does not want; it becomes

the most played in a short time but the sales are very small."
With his Valentine's Day number, Berlin had failed to heed his
own warning.

But just as "Be Careful" began its slide, extraordinary news
began to filter into Berlin's New York headquarters. Suddenly,
without a lick of "exploitation" to nudge it along, "White
Christmas" was selling like a hit. On September 19, *Billboard*
reported that Bing Crosby's recording of "White Christmas"
was being "gobbled up"—this despite the fact that Berlin,
determined to hold off on promoting the song until the Christmas season had begun in earnest, had forbidden radio "air-
plugging" of the number and had "not encouraged its sale."

Sales of "White Christmas" sheet music were just as brisk.
Every day, reports from sheet music jobbers reached Berlin's
staff in New York: stores couldn't stock "White Christmas"
quickly enough; another twenty thousand copies were needed,
immediately. Louis Dreyfus, the head of Berlin's U.K. operation, informed his boss that the song would be the biggest the
London office had ever handled. " 'Christmas' is our number
one song without any plugs," Berlin exulted. The leaves on
Central Park trees hadn't yet turned, and already the public
was clamoring for his snow song. It was, he declared, a "sensation."

Grizzled music business veterans were floored by the
song's reception. On October 7, Berlin, in Washington, D.C.,
with the *This Is the Army* troupe, received a letter from
Emanuel Sacks, the head of A&R at Columbia Records. The
previous evening, Sacks had stepped into a Times Square
nightclub, the Piccadilly Grill, and watched the Three Suns, a

popular harmony group, perform Berlin's "unusual song." "Never in all my years in the business," Sacks wrote, "did I witness such an enthusiastic response to a song. It seemed to affect everyone in the audience (including me), and the boys had to do several encores." That same week, with Crosby's Decca 78 continuing to sell at a furious pace and a new recording of the song by the Freddy Martin Orchestra looking formidable, *Billboard* pronounced "White Christmas" "one of the most phenomenal hits in the history of the music business."

As the tune's snowballing record and sheet-music sales turned "White Christmas" into Berlin's biggest hit since "Always" in the mid-1920s, the songwriter's chief concern was that the song not exhaust its popularity before the Christmas season began in earnest. Worried that if the tune petered out early, its chances of turning into a "hardy perennial" would be spoiled, Berlin found himself in an absurd position: scheming to stop "White Christmas" from becoming *too* big a hit. "Irving Berlin is pretty upset over the too-frequent plugging of his song," reported one gossip columnist.

But the juggernaut would not be slowed. "Neither calendar makers nor the publisher could hold it back for long," exclaimed *Billboard*'s October 31 issue, the week that Crosby's record first topped its charts. Scarcely anything else was being played on the nation's jukeboxes, the magazine reported. " 'Christmas' covers the coin photo network like a blanket of snow and pulls those nickels as if old Santa himself were throwing the pitch. All that's left . . . is to stock up on platters and change them as they wear out."

Soon Berlin stopped fretting about "White Christmas":

there was no danger it would fizzle. On November 2, he wrote a boastful letter to Mark Sandrich: " 'White Christmas' is the talk of the music business. There are only so many of these kind of songs in a songwriter's system. They are the milestones, all the others are 'filler-ins,' even if they become popular. . . . I know you don't mind me going on about 'White Christmas' in this manner."

As Christmas, 1942, drew closer, the song was ubiquitous. A political cartoon in the *New York Post* depicted Hitler, curled up in swastika-covered pajamas, "Dreaming of a White Christmas" on the snowy Russian front. In mid-November, weather forecasters began weighing the odds that "Irving Berlin's dream" would come true six weeks hence. *Time* magazine proclaimed the song the biggest smash of Berlin's "hit-studded" career and speculated that its success alone might reverse the fortunes of the slumping sheet-music industry. "For the first time in many year," a Baltimore newspaper declared, the nation's sheet music sellers would "not have to throw the stuff under the counter this Christmas and display teddy bears and musical gadgets instead." America's first full year at war had had its share of pop culture sensations—the continuing popularity of Glenn Miller, Jimmy Dorsey, and other "sweet" swing orchestras, the Academy Award–winning *Casablanca*—but nothing had been as unanimously embraced as "White Christmas." Its appeal even transcended racial barriers—Bing Crosby's record became the first by a white artist to chart on *Billboard*'s Harlem Hit Parade.

An editorial in the *Christian Science Monitor* marveled at the "White Christmas" phenomenon:

Irving Berlin's "White Christmas" . . . has sung its way into practically every home and heart in the country. . . . Snatches of it may be heard on almost any street in America. . . . No one seems to be able to explain just why. Even Mr. Berlin himself is puzzled.

But Berlin was less puzzled than flabbergasted. He had never seen a song become a hit in this curious fashion. Berlin was right: *history makes songs*. For the groundswell that was sweeping "White Christmas" up the charts had begun with an audience that no song-plugger's hard sell could reach. "Something amazing is happening to this song," Berlin had announced one night at the family dinner table. "The boys overseas are buying it."

In no sector of American society had the war mobilization that followed Pearl Harbor been undertaken with more furious dispatch than in Tin Pan Alley. According to one estimate, more than one thousand war-themed songs were submitted to song-publishing firms that terrible week. Just days after the attack, the nation's airwaves and dance halls resounded with war songs of the most strident sort: "You're a Sap, Mr. Jap," "We'll Nip the Nipponese," "We're Gonna Change the Map of the Jap," "The Japs Don't Have a Chinaman's Chance," "Let's Take a Rap at the Jap," "We're Gonna Find a Fellow Who's Very, Very Yellow, and Beat Him Till He's Red, White and Blue."

In their chest-thumping belligerence, such songs recalled

the tunes about whipping the kaiser that appeared at the out-set of the Great War. More than two decades later, World War I's most famous songs—"It's a Long Way to Tipperary," "Keep the Home Fires Burning," and especially George M. Cohan's "Over There"—were still fondly recalled as the anthems that had propelled American boys through the smoldering battle-fields of that "marching war." It was a sign of Tin Pan Alley's cultural stature that with the nation once again engaged in an epic struggle, the need for appropriate popular songs quickly came to be regarded as a matter of pressing national concern.

"What this country needs is a good five-cent war song," said Pennsylvania congressman J. Parnell Thomas. "The nation is literally crying out for a good, peppy marching song, something with plenty of zip, ginger, and fire." Thomas was not alone in this opinion. Military officials, newspaper pundits, clergymen, and business leaders all joined in calling on Tin Pan Alley to supply inspiring war anthems. William B. Lewis, head of the Office of War Information's Radio Division, com-plained that Americans were not being "exposed to enough worthy war songs on radio" and implored the music industry to banish "drivel" from the airwaves. "Songwriters ought to put their muses to the grindstone," wrote Damon Runyon in his nationally syndicated column, "and turn out things that would reflect the seriousness of war." Eager to do its wartime part, the pop song industry scrambled together a Music War Com-mittee, headed by Oscar Hammerstein II, and announced its intention to find a song to "do for this war what George M. Cohan's 'Over There' did for the last one."

But by the autumn of 1942, with the first anniversary of

Pearl Harbor approaching, an "Over There" for the new war had yet to emerge. Even Berlin's *This Is the Army* score had failed to yield an appropriate musical rallying cry. A handful of war-themed numbers had become minor hits. There were boisterous marches ("Remember Pearl Harbor," "We Did It Before and We Can Do It Again") and war-themed tear-jerkers ("When the Lights Go On Again All Over the World," "He Wears a Pair of Silver Wings"). But most of the successful war songs were novelties: "Boogie Woogie Bugle Boy," "Goodbye, Mama, I'm Off to Yokohama," "Send a Great Big Salami to Your Boyfriend in the Army (and He'll Bring Home the Bacon to You)," and most popular of all, Spike Jones's "Der Fuehrer's Face," a raucous Nazi lampoon that appeared in the Walt Disney animated short *Donald Duck in Nutzi Land*—hardly the songs of high-minded patriotic purpose that everyone seemed to be demanding. "Drivel" still ruled the charts.

It was at just that time, in September 1942, that "the boys overseas" began clamoring for copies of Irving Berlin's Christmas ballad. The manner in which "White Christmas" had reached American uniformed men underscored a pivotal change in American popular music. Throughout the 1930s, commercial records had become an increasingly important presence in popular culture; at the turn of the new decade, with the nation's economy bouncing back, tens of millions of discs were being sold each year. Since commercial radio was dominated by live band performers, the market for those records was evenly split between home phonograph players and the country's latest rage in cheap public entertainment, jukeboxes.

The war mobilization that took millions of American men out of the workforce and into the military did not spare the music industry. Dance bands were depleted of their players. The impact of this musical talent drain was felt not just in dance halls but at radio networks, whose studio bands had heretofore provided most of the music heard on the nation's airwaves. Radio broadcasters had resisted playing canned music, but now, caught shorthanded, they had little choice.

Commercial radio was by far the biggest promotional venue for pop songs, and the wartime opening of its doors to recorded music was destined to transform popular music. An estimated 75 percent of American radio programming in the 1940s came from records. Though live radio broadcasts of big-name stars still enjoyed immense popularity—notably, Crosby's *Kraft Music Hall* program—a new type of radio star, the disc jockey, was coming into his own. Among the most prominent was Martin Block, whose nationally broadcast program had a title that summed up the shift from live to canned music: *Make Believe Ballroom.*

It was Crosby's Decca recording that carried "White Christmas" to American troops and began the song's astounding chart-topping run. The record reached American soldiers in a variety of ways. It aired on Armed Forces Radio request programs. It was played on jukeboxes in USO halls and PX stores. It arrived in the recreation kits that the military had developed in recognition of the importance of music in boosting troop morale. (In Kurt Vonnegut's *Mother Night,* a collector of these kits winds up with twenty-six copies of Crosby's "White Christmas.") We can never know how the first domino fell—in what PX jukebox a GI first dropped his nickel and ordered up Crosby's new tune, whose care package from home included a Decca 78. But by mid-September, fully three months before the holiday it celebrated, the demand of overseas soldiers for "White Christmas" had reached such a pitch that it was being felt on the music charts, and the ardor for the song was spreading to the home front thousands of miles away.

The previous spring, Berlin had tried to turn "White Christmas" into a war song. In May, he had told his business partner Saul Bornstein that he was at work on a "White Christmas" war verse—"a new verse that will fit these times." The effort proved fruitless: though he struggled for weeks, Berlin recalled, "new words would not come."

He needn't have bothered: the song was perfect for "these times" the way it was. Christmas, 1942, was the first that millions of Americans would spend away from home. " 'White Christmas' brings memories to almost every American," said the *Christian Science Monitor*, and to soldiers hearing Bing Crosby's sleepy-voiced recording in boot-camp barracks in Georgia, Mississippi, and California, in USO halls in Great Britain, aboard naval battleships making treacherous North Atlantic passages, those memories were particularly moving. Above all, the song appealed to servicemen in the warmest climes—posted on Guadalcanal in the Pacific, heading into combat in North Africa—who faced the prospect of an unwintry holiday season. A poem in the *New York Herald Tribune,* entitled "With Apologies to Irving Berlin," imagined the feelings "White Christmas" evoked in the "boys in the tropics":

Men are longing for a white Christmas
In scorching lands where snow is never seen
Recalling rime upon their red-cheeked faces
In jungles where the very air is green.
Who will wake up on a hot Christmas morning,
Homesick for skates and sled, the freighted branch;
Sweating beneath the sky's incessant burning,
Will long to tread white fields, to hear snow crunch.

Nearly a year after Pearl Harbor, America's wartime anthem had materialized, in the improbable shape of a Christmas tune. The appeal of "White Christmas" was about more than sweat-soaked soldiers longing to break out the toboggan. In the song's melancholic yearning for Christmases past, listeners heard the expression of their own nostalgia for peacetime. "White Christmas" was no "Over There." It was an "over here," a vision of home-front serenity, of the imperiled "American way of life" that the nation was fighting to defend. "When Irving Berlin set 120,000,000 people dreaming of a White Christmas," wrote the *Buffalo Courier-Express,* "he provided a forcible reminder that we are fighting for the right to dream and memories to dream about."

On November 21, "White Christmas" began a precedent-shattering ten-week-long run at the top of the Hit Parade chart. It overtook a martial tune to which the country had never really warmed, Frank Loesser's "Praise the Lord and Pass the Ammunition." Loesser's song, with its lusty major chords, gung ho oaths, and images of gunners and fighter pilots, struck all the right war-song postures; under orders from government officials, radio stations bludgeoned it into popular favor, playing it tens of times daily.

"White Christmas" never mentioned the war, yet it was the more potent wartime anthem, inciting patriotism in its most primal form: homesickness. Wartime homesickness was an affliction experienced by millions of Americans, even those on the home front. According to one estimate, nearly one in every ten Americans—12 million people—made a permanent move to another state during World War II. The farm population declined dramatically; urban and suburban populations swelled. Wrenched from their normal lives and the places they had known, separated from their sweethearts, their husbands, their wives, their parents, their children, Americans naturally found themselves responding to the wistful sentiments in Berlin's Christmas home song.

Christmas, 1942, was fast approaching. It had been a difficult twelve months. Early in the year, U.S. forces had suffered harsh defeats in battles in the Philippines and the Java Sea. Heavy American casualties were taken in the naval triumph at Guadalcanal. Just before Christmas week, Americans finally had cause for cheer. Eddie Rickenbacker, the president of Eastern Airlines, a former race-car driver and a fighter-pilot hero of World War I, had joined the air force again, even though he was over fifty years old. In October his B-17 had crashed several hundred miles north of Samoa, setting him and his crew of seven men adrift on rubber rafts. Now came the word that Rickenbacker and company had been found— they'd spent twenty-three days in the "watery wastes," their sole provisions four oranges and two fishing lines, yet all but one man had survived. It was, headlines cried, a "Christmas miracle."

During Christmas week, Berlin found himself autographing the millionth copy of "White Christmas" sheet music, to be auctioned off for the benefit of war charities. The song had sold more sheet music than any since the advent of big-time radio nearly twenty years earlier. And with sales of Bing Crosby's recording topping 2 million, "White Christmas" was on its way to becoming the best-selling record in history. Yet listeners who tuned in to Crosby's Christmas Eve *Kraft Music Hall* broadcast to hear the singer croon the nation's number one song were disappointed: he sang "Silent Night" and "Adeste Fideles," but not "White Christmas." The song's broadcast rights had been secured by another NBC radio act, comedy duo Abbott and Costello.

That Christmas, Berlin was in Detroit with *This Is the Army*'s touring troupe. Ellin and the girls joined him for the holiday, and on Christmas Eve day, a group of newspaper reporters and photographers were invited to watch the Berlins trim their holiday tree. This banal promotional stunt took a more interesting turn when Berlin sat down at the piano for an impromptu performance of his Christmas hit. As he sang—in what one of the reporters called his "reedy, quavering croon"—Berlin noticed his audience's discomfort with the introductory "Beverly Hills, L.A." verse. As soon as the press event ended, Berlin phoned Saul Bornstein in New York: "I want you to cut the verse out of the sheet music of 'White Christmas.' From now on, that song goes without a verse. That's an order."

On Christmas Day, the Berlins awoke to find gray Detroit squatting beneath a sky of falling snow. Midwesterners could be forgiven for believing that Berlin had some kind of meteorological omniscience: in the nation's heartland, Christmas, 1942, was white. "We observed with considerable pleasure that Irving Berlin's dream of a white Christmas finally did come true," proclaimed the *Detroit Free Press* a couple of days later. "We're certainly glad that everything turned out all right."

When "White Christmas" toppled "Praise the Lord and Pass the Ammunition," it announced the triumph of sentiment over Sturm und Drang: during World War II, ballads ruled the charts. The biggest hits of the war were songs that addressed traumatic parting, brooded over the years and miles that separated lovers, looked forward to reunions: "As Time Goes By," "I'll Be Seeing You," "It's Been a Long, Long Time," "We'll Meet Again," "You'd Be So Nice to Come Home To." To those ballads' potent sentimentality, "White Christmas" added the special pathos associated with the holiday. Berlin understood the holiday's emotional force. "The boys in the South Pacific must have read into ['White Christmas'] cranberry sauce, roast turkey, Christmas carols, the family around the hearthside, a glowing Christmas tree," the songwriter recalled years later.

This catalog of Christmas associations, like Berlin's Christmas song, is conspicuously bereft of religious imagery. But "White Christmas" wasn't just a Jew's capricious gloss on the holiday. In the first decades of the twentieth century, American society had undergone a radical secularization; now, the wartime emphasis on national unity was fostering even greater ecumenical feeling. It was the World War II U.S. military that, in an effort to forge interreligious bonding among soldiers, gave us the term "Judeo-Christian tradition." The fact that America was at war with a fascist enemy notorious for its religious intolerance made the need for displays of secular unity all the more urgent.

The celebration of the American Christmas—that magically sanctified and ostentatiously irreligious holiday—became a kind of patriotic act. A few prominent rabbis even advocated Jews keeping Christmas; not coincidentally, it was during this same period that Chanukah, a relatively minor holiday on the Jewish calendar, gained the status of the "Jewish Christmas," an effort not just to preserve a distinctive Jewish identity but to hitch together the two festivals in a display of the nation's cultural oneness. Christmas had long been the de facto national holiday, but now President Roosevelt made it explicit. "It is significant that tomorrow—Christmas Day—our plants and factories will be still," he told the nation in his Christmas Eve, 1942, fireside chat. "That is not true of the other holidays. . . . On all other holidays the work goes on, gladly, for the winning of the war. So Christmas Day becomes the only holiday of the year."

The "national anthem" for the newly consecrated national holiday was, of course, Berlin's song. And while Reform rabbis were sanctioning Jewish Christmas celebration, Christian clergy were bringing a Jew's Christmas carol into their houses of worship. On the Sunday before Christmas in 1943, Carl S. Winters, the pastor of the First Baptist Church in Oak Park, Illinois, delivered a sermon that meditated on the significance of "White Christmas" during wartime:

> It wasn't just snow [the singer] was dreaming about. It was everything that is written in the soul of man that longs for the beauty and loveliness and the mystery embodied in the Christmas story. . . . When I say "White Christmas" I don't mean the white of snow alone, I mean the white of purity in a world of bestiality; I mean the white of peace in a world of war; I mean the white of hope in an hour of despair; I mean the white of the light of truth in the heart of every man in a time of blackouts. . . . To many people this is not a white Christmas; it is a red Christmas. They see blood in the snow. They see it soaked in the sands of the desert. They see it caked on the clothing of soldiers. . . . But I think we should still dream of a white Christmas of peace on earth and goodwill among men. . . . My friends, I say that more than at any other time, now is when we need to dream of a white Christmas on the world front and in our human hearts.

"White Christmas" returned to the top of the Hit Parade that year and would do so again in 1944. The song was eclipsing all of Berlin's standards and was on its way to becoming the single most valuable copyright in the history of American popular music. Berlin pronounced "White Christmas" his second-favorite song—only "God Bless America" edged it out in the songwriter's affections.

Particularly satisfying was the approval of the constituency that had made the song a hit in the first place. Today, World War II GIs are mythologized as idealistic warriors who fought to save the world from fascism and to preserve democracy. But polls taken at the time reveal that only 13 percent of GIs could name three of Roosevelt's Four Freedoms, and only one in twenty fought for clearly defined idealistic reasons. Above all, American soldiers fought "to get the goddamn thing over and come home," as one marine at Guadalcanal put it. With its mystical vision of the home to which they longed to return, "White Christmas" was, for many American soldiers, a "why we fight" anthem that was true to life.

During their wartime travels, Berlin and Crosby experienced firsthand the song's powerful effect. Crosby made frequent trips overseas as a member of the USO's entertainment troupes. Wherever he went, no matter the season, he was asked to sing "White Christmas." "So many young people were away and they'd hear this song . . . and it would really affect them," Crosby remembered. "I sang it many times in Europe in the field for the soldiers. They'd holler for it; they'd demand and I'd sing it and they'd all cry. It was really sad."

Once, Crosby was entertaining a paratroop unit in France. Before the performance, the singer was approached by a gruff, square-jawed sergeant. "You gonna sing 'White Christmas'?" he asked. Crosby assured him he would.

"Well, in that case, I guess I'll duck out," the sergeant said.

"I think you'll like the other numbers," Crosby replied. "Why not stick around?"

"I like the song all right," the sergeant explained. "But I'll listen from behind the portable kitchen. It's no good for the men's morale to see their sergeant crying."

That sergeant wasn't the only soldier who worried that the song would overwhelm his emotions. Lyell Thompson, a squad leader in the army's Ninety-ninth Infantry Division, recalls that his unit imposed a ban on singing or humming "White Christmas" during the six weeks it spent in foxholes on the German-Belgian border over the Christmas season of 1944. On the one hand, the last thing soldiers shivering in the snowy Ardennes wanted to do was to sing an ode to snow-filled woods; but Thompson admits that the real reason for the ban was the soldiers' fear of getting choked up singing Berlin's song, marking another holiday spent far from home.

British troops also responded to "White Christmas." During Christmas, 1942, Edna Long, an army nurse from Melrose, Massachusetts, was put in charge of organizing a yuletide concert at the Salvation Army canteen in Ahmadnagar, India, for British soldiers who were passing through en route to a showdown with the Japanese in Burma. An English soldier suggested that Long allow "Chips," a nineteen-year-old enlistee from Yorkshire, to perform at the concert. "You ought to get Chips to sing 'White Christmas,'" she was told. "He's tops."

On the evening of the concert, Chips showed up clutching "White Christmas" sheet music he'd sent for in Bombay. He was a slight, fair-haired, blue-eyed boy; there was a lilt in his tenor voice that betrayed his northern English origins. After hearing him rehearse, Long decided his number should be the last of the evening.

The canteen was packed and crowds pressed in at the door from the outside. Though the hall held only five hundred, when the audience joined in singing "Joy to the World" and "Good King Wenceslas," it sounded, Long remembered, as if "all ten thousand men were out there in the dark singing with us."

Finally, it was Chips's turn. He lumbered to the platform in his boots, fumbling with his coat buttons. The crown tittered. But "as soon as Chips began to sing," Long recalled, "a hush fell over that crowded, stuffy hall, and something crept over the faces of the men in that audience that I had never seen before. They weren't weak or sentimental. Many of them had been through Dunkirk and Madagascar or escaped from Singapore or Rangoon. But as Chips sang, the grim, hard lines on their faces softened and a new light came into their eyes. . . . When he finished, there was a long pause and then the burst of applause was deafening."

The men pushed Chips back on the stage and demanded that he sing the tune another time. The canteen was silent again. This time Chips changed the lyrics slightly: "I'm praying for a white Christmas . . ." Many men in the audience broke down and wept.

Chips slipped out the back door following his encore, and Long never saw him again. In January, his division moved toward Burma; in April, some units were sent to Arakan, where they were "defeated by the Japanese and jungle fever." Long was later reunited with one of the wounded from the division, a man who had sung in a quartet that evening. Chips had been killed in the first week of the campaign at Arakan.

"Chips was always talking about getting back to Yorkshire for next Christmas," the soldier told her. He had sung "White Christmas" "all the way to the Burma border," the soldier reported. "He was singing it when the Japs finally got him at Arakan."

During his years-long tour with *This Is the Army*, Berlin frequently came face-to-face with the passions that his song ignited. Often, after performances of the show, audiences would implore Berlin to come back to the stage to sing his Christmas tune.

On Christmas Eve, 1944, a group of GIs in Hollandia, New Guinea, returned the favor. Berlin and his company arrived in Hollandia that evening; they were slated to give a Christmas performance the next day. Normally when Berlin arrived for an engagement, he was given VIP treatment—whisked away with the local military brass. But that night, to the songwriter's delight, he was invited to spend Christmas Eve rubbing elbows with local GIs at the enlisted men's club.

At three minutes after midnight the GIs rose and said, "Let's sing a song for Irving Berlin." "As one man, they sang 'White Christmas,'" Berlin remembered. "I'd never heard it sung so well. Their gesture marked the Christmas I can't forget." The next day, Berlin would get another treat: as he whizzed past in a military van, the songwriter overheard local

New Guinean tribesmen singing "White Christmas" in their strange native tongue.

Nineteen forty-five was a year of tumult and triumph. In February, with the Allies on the verge of victory, Roosevelt, Churchill, and Stalin met at the Yalta Conference. Two months later, on April 12, Roosevelt died; that same week, the Allies liberated the concentration camps at Belsen and Buchenwald. On April 30, Hitler committed suicide in his Berlin bunker. On May 7, Germany surrendered. On August 6, the *Enola Gay* dropped an atomic bomb on Hiroshima, Japan, killing an estimated 140,000 Japanese and flattening four square miles. On September 2, at a ceremony aboard the battleship USS *Missouri*, Japan formally surrendered. America was coming home for Christmas.

For the first time in four years, Americans celebrated the holiday in a world at peace. But some things didn't change. Crosby's "White Christmas" was the year's top-selling record; for the fourth Christmas running, the song was perched atop the Hit Parade charts. It would return to that position the following year, and the year after that.

On March 19, 1947, Bing Crosby returned to Decca Studios for an unusual session. Decca's master dub plate of "White Christmas," whose sales now numbered well over 5 million, had become so worn that the company was forced to rerecord the song. The same crew that had been present for the original recording session—the John Scott Trotter Orchestra, the Ken Darby singers—was reassembled, and the original arrangement was aped to the last detail.

But the keen-eared could detect some differences. Crosby,

who, with typical nonchalance, recut his most famous performance in a single take, had a deeper, more darkly burnished voice now; and he made some minor changes in emphasis and intonation. (Gone was that wistful mordent in the song's second syllable: "*dream*ing.") In the ensuing decades, as the old records got scratched and 78 rpm turntables were put out with the trash, this remake became the definitive Crosby "White Christmas." It was only in 1998, when MCA/Decca rereleased the weather-beaten 1942 original on a double-CD compilation of Crosby's Christmas recordings, that listeners could once again hear, through a small snowstorm of static, the sound that had enthralled a war-torn world.

8

Let It Snow

✦

"It's beginning to look a lot like Christmas":
the cast of *Irving Berlin's White Christmas*, 1954.
Courtesy of The Irving Berlin Music Company.

The radio was playing "Easter Parade" and I thought, But this is Jewish genius on par with the Ten Commandments. God gave Moses the Ten Commandments and then He gave Irving Berlin "Easter Parade" and "White Christmas." The two holidays that celebrate the divinity of Christ—the divinity that's the very heart of the Jewish rejection of Christianity—and what does Irving Berlin brilliantly do? He de-Christs them both! Easter turns into a fashion show and Christmas into a holiday about snow. . . . He turns their religion into schlock. But nicely! Nicely! So nicely the goyim don't even know what hit 'em. . . . Bing Crosby replaces Jesus as the beloved Son of God. . . . And is that so disgraceful a means of defusing the enmity of centuries? If schlockified Christianity is Christianity cleansed of Jew hatred, then three cheers for schlock. If supplanting Jesus Christ with snow can enable my people to cozy up to Christmas, then let it snow, let it snow, let it snow!

—PHILIP ROTH,
Operation Shylock

WHEN "WHITE CHRISTMAS" entered the Lucky Strike Hit Parade countdown on October 17, 1942, at number seven, it marked the first time a Christmas song had ever charted in the weekly survey. The following year, when the song returned to the chart, it had company: "I'll Be Home for Christmas," a ballad cowritten by Walter Kent, Kim Gannon, and Buck Ram, was the season's new yuletide hit. Although its melody—rising and plunging over a chord progression rich in luminous minor sixths—had a melancholy radiance all its own, "I'll Be Home for Christmas" was blatantly a "White Christmas" knockoff. The song was introduced by a stately Bing Crosby recording; its lyrics—a pledge to return to a snowy Christmas homestead, "if only in my dreams"—tapped into the same strain of wartime holiday yearning.

"I'll Be Home for Christmas" was only the most successful of several holiday songs that Tin Pan Alley's publishers were pushing on the first anniversary of Berlin's triumph. Music industry bible *Billboard* took note of the trend: "Kringle Jingles Ring the Bell—Xmas Time Is Music Time," the magazine declared. In the past, *Billboard* reported, songwriters had avoided "laboring over holiday songs because previous experience had convinced them that the tunes are generally played on that day alone and cleared off the retail counters the day after." Now, in the wake of "White Christmas," Tin Pan Alley had realized its Christmas numbers could become "all-timers . . . modern classics," to which the public would return year after year, generating annual "servings of Yule Day gravy."

A pattern was established that would continue over the next decade: each year brought "White Christmas" back to the nation's airwaves and music charts; each year, dozens of new would-be holiday standards flooded the market. Some of the new tunes stuck. Nineteen forty-four introduced "Have Yourself a Merry Little Christmas," another ballad whose lachrymose sentiments and minor chords traded on wartime sadness. The next year, "Let It Snow! Let It Snow! Let It Snow!" captured the high spirits of a victorious nation celebrating a postwar Christmas.

By 1952, a decade after the debut of "White Christmas," Tin Pan Alley had given the country a new canon of holiday pop tunes that, seemingly instantly, had acquired cultural stature on par with Handel's *Messiah*, traditional Christmas hymns, and nineteenth-century secular carols like "Jingle Bells" and "Deck the Halls." In addition to "White Christmas," "I'll Be Home for Christmas," "Have Yourself a Merry Little Christmas," and "Let It Snow! Let It Snow! Let It Snow!" there were "The Christmas Song (Chestnuts Roasting on an Open Fire)," "Rudolph the Red-Nosed Reindeer," "Silver Bells," "Sleigh Ride," "Frosty the Snowman," and "It's Beginning to Look a Lot Like Christmas." The Christmas music craze even swept a pair of Tin Pan Alley also-rans—"Winter Wonderland" and "Santa Claus Is Comin' to Town," both nonstarters when they were published in 1934—onto the Hit Parade and into the Christmas carol pantheon.

But the Christmas entertainment boom wasn't limited to popular song. In 1944, M-G-M released *Meet Me in St. Louis,* a musical set in the turn-of-the-century Midwest that, like *Hol-*

iday Inn, valorized Christmas as a bastion of old-fashioned values and made a sentimental yuletide ballad ("Have Yourself a Merry Little Christmas") its centerpiece song. This was followed by a trio of Christmas films—*It's a Wonderful Life* (1946), *Miracle on 34th Street* (1947), *The Bishop's Wife* (1947)—whose repeated television airings in subsequent years established them as fixtures of the national Christmas festival.

It was no accident that this explosion in Christmas-themed entertainment occurred during and just after the war. The wartime emphasis on ecumenicalism solidified Christmas's stature as the preeminent American festival; and the holiday's exalted place in the national imagination was matched by its importance to the economy. The Christmas shopping season—the weeks between Thanksgiving and December 25—had long proven vital to the health of the nation's retail sector. In 1939, President Roosevelt, aiming to spur continued economic recovery, ordered Thanksgiving moved from November 30 to November 23; in 1941, Congress altered the calendar permanently, enacting a law that moved Thanksgiving to the fourth, as opposed to the last, Thursday in November, guaranteeing an annual four-week shopping season.

Tin Pan Alley and Hollywood would join in reaping the Christmas sugarplums. Together with print advertising, books, and other mass-media products, the new Christmas songs and films consolidated the imagery, language, and lore of the modern holiday, allowing millions of Americans to experience what historian Penne Restad has called "a Christmas more uniform and secular than any preceding it." Though their tone varied wildly—ranging from the melodrama of *It's a Wonderful Life,* Frank Capra's dark gloss on the Scrooge story, to the garishly corny "Frosty the Snowman"—they all emphasized "the Christmas spirit," that vaguely supernatural mixture of Santa Claus, seasonal cheer, brightly wrapped presents, snowfall, family, and "goodwill towards men." The new pop Christmas icons had a distinctively American flavor. "Rudolph the Red-Nosed Reindeer"—originally a narrative poem distributed by the Montgomery Ward department store as a promotional gimmick—was a Horatio Alger fable transplanted to the North Pole: the story of a plucky misfit who turns his handicap (a "very shiny nose") into an asset, succeeds famously (in making Santa's sleigh run on time), and wins the acclaim of the ages ("Rudolph the Red-Nosed Reindeer, you'll go down in history!").

Above all, the Christmas movies and tunes were relentless in their hallowing of the past. Like "White Christmas," they offered a vision of the holiday as a nostalgia trip: a journey back to a better, simpler time. "Here we are, as in olden days / Happy golden days of yore," went the key lines of "Have Yourself a Merry Little Christmas," delivered by Judy Garland in *Meet Me in St. Louis* with a maudlin catch in her voice. The new, aggressively nostalgic Christmas entertainment embodied a central paradox of commercial Christmas culture: they were modern, big-city, mass-media products that sold the holiday as a retreat from, and rebuke to, high-tech urban modernity—a trick that seems the essence of city-slicker salesmanship.

In the years since, the songs and movies themselves have

become objects of the holiday nostalgia that they depict. When America Online conducted a poll in the winter of 2001, asking its users to identify their favorite Christmas songs, respondents invariably identified those that spurred reveries for Christmases past. "White Christmas," in particular, seemed to fuel nostalgia. "It wouldn't be an old-fashioned Christmas without Bing singing 'White Christmas,' " wrote one AOL user; " 'White Christmas' reminds me of old-time Christmas. Stockings by the fireplace, the family house, the good old days."

Such sentiments are a reminder that Christmas is an ad hoc creation. From the holiday's inception, celebrants have had a fluid sense of Christmas tradition. Although the early church fathers agreed that Jesus was born in the spring, when the Roman Church began to observe a Feast of the Nativity in the fourth century of the Common Era, it placed the holiday on December 25, the date of the winter solstice on the Julian calendar, in order to compete with the increasingly popular pagan festival of Saturnalia. Ever since, revelers have continued to improvise Christmas tradition, remaking the holiday's rites and icons to suit their circumstances. Think of the centuries-long evolution that turned Nicholas, a fourth-century monk from Myra in Asia Minor revered for his charitable good works, into Clement Clarke Moore's "right jolly old elf," who pilots a reindeer-drawn sleigh, fills stockings with candied fruit, and ascends chimneys with a nod of his head. As numerous scholars have shown, the traditional American Christmas—the celebration of faith and family, of gift-giving and tree-trimming and carol-singing—was a creation of the nineteenth century, a domestication of what had become an increasingly raucous carnival holiday marked by drunken "misrule" and violent outbursts of social-class resentment.

The customs of that new domestic-centered holiday were in many ways the creation of the marketplace. We might envision a time when every New Englander trudged through snowy woods to chop down his Christmas tree, but the German tradition of bringing an evergreen into the home at Christmastime only became widespread in the United States when canny businessmen began to haul trees into urban centers for sale in open-air markets. Similarly, the image of Santa Claus wasn't fixed in the public imagination until political cartoonist Thomas Nast's sketches of a plump, ruddy-cheeked figure first appeared in *Harper's Weekly* in 1863. Today, when we decry the commercialization of Christmas, we scarcely realize that the "traditional" holiday was invented by the commercial entities we malign for defiling it.

An even sharper irony surrounds the Christmas songs and films that continue to shape Americans' sense of Christmas tradition: they were, largely, the creation of Jews. "White Christmas" is merely the most illustrious example of the phenomenon. As songwriters, music publishers, record label executives, movie studio heads, and screenwriters, Jews had a hand in virtually every major midcentury Christmas song and film. Bing Crosby recorded "Silent Night" only after being bullied into it by the Chicago-reared son of Ukrainian Jewish immigrants. *Miracle on 34th Street* was released by Adolph Zukor's Twentieth Century-Fox Studios and produced by William Perlberg. "The Christmas Song," that ode to "old-time carols being sung by a choir," was written by a pair of Jewish teenagers, Mel Tormé and Robert Wells Levinson. "Rudolph the Red-Nosed Reindeer" was composed by another Jewish New Yorker, the songwriter Johnny Marks, who became such a specialist in seasonal novelties that he named his song-publishing firm St. Nicholas Music.

Neil Gabler has observed that the Jewish movie moguls who invented Hollywood had a "neurotic" reverence for the American majority culture; they pursued their Americanization with an almost pathological fervor, Gabler says, waging "war against their own pasts." It is tempting to read the role Jews played in the promotion of Christmas entertainment in a similar light. Gabler's profile would seem to fit Irving Berlin rather well; certainly, "White Christmas" ranks as a particularly audacious assault by Berlin—who learned his first songs in synagogue at the side of his cantor father—on his Jewish past.

But Berlin fought on two fronts: while he forsook his religious heritage, he made a subtler, more mischievous conquest of the American imagination. In this respect, Philip Roth's outrageous fictional doppelgänger in *Operation Shylock*, who sings the "Jewish genius" of "White Christmas" and likens the song's power to an "Israeli nuclear reactor," offers as good a take as any on Jews and Christmas music.

In an age of post-melting-pot identity politics, we might regard the Jewish creation of Christmas culture with a mixture of bewilderment and scorn. But this view misses the impishness of a feat like "White Christmas" the sheer chutzpah that compelled a refugee from a pogrom-scourged corner of Siberia—no stranger to the subtler American forms of anti-Semitic prejudice—to write a Christmas anthem that buried all traces of the holiday's Christian origins beneath three feet of driven snow. The Rothian gloss on Berlin's song suggests a Seussian subtitle: "White Christmas," or, How the Jews Stole Christmas.

On the other hand, "White Christmas" and other holiday songs represent a Jewish triumph of a less grandiose sort. In the decades since the release of "White Christmas," the music industry has reaped extravagant, multibillion-dollar profits from sales of Christmas tunes. One measure of the Christmas music phenomenon is the perennial popularity of holiday theme albums. The earliest such LP was, not surprisingly, Bing Crosby's *Merry Christmas*, a collection of his Decca Christmas sides (including, of course, "White Christmas") that was the top-selling album in the history of the record industry in the pre-compact-disc era. After the release of Crosby's LP, Christmas theme albums became ubiquitous: nearly every major singer of the prerock era—from Frank Sinatra to Nat King Cole to Ella Fitzgerald to Tony Bennett—recorded at least one collection of holiday songs.

The trend has continued in the age of rock. Ten of the Recording Industry Association of America's twenty-five all-time top-selling artists—all of them rock-era stalwarts—have released Christmas LPs. Today, holiday albums remain de rigueur for a certain breed of multi-platinum pop, R&B, and country performer. Recent years have seen the release of Christmas collections by N Sync, the Backstreet Boys,

9

Old Songs

Berlin in his last photo session, 1974.
He was 86 years old and would live another decade and a half.
Courtesy of The Irving Berlin Music Company.

I do hope I'll see you this year. It'll be fun to talk about the *present day screwed* up *nudie rudie* foul show business. It's so overloaded with crummy crap I just won't go to see anything anymore.

—FRED ASTAIRE,
in a letter to Irving Berlin, 1970

Another birthday and you're almost in tears;
Another birthday and you're counting the years.

—IRVING BERLIN,
"Old Men"

T HE POSTWAR phase of Berlin's career began promisingly. When Jerome Kern died suddenly in November of 1945, Berlin was persuaded to take over his late friend's scorewriting duties for a musical based on the life of Annie Oakley, the gunslinging "little Miss Sure Shot" of the 1890s Wild West. The result was *Annie Get Your Gun,* whose period setting reflected popular culture's continued love affair with folksy Americana and provided a vivid backdrop for a handful of Berlin's best songs: "Doin' What Comes Naturally," "They Say

It's Wonderful," "The Girl That I Marry," "You Can't Get a Man with a Gun," "Lost in His Arms," "There's No Business Like Show Business." The cleverest of the bunch was the "answer song" "Anything You Can Do," whose haughty one-upmanship may have caught Berlin's mood: once again, the songwriter had kept pace with changing times, meeting the challenge of Rodgers and Hammerstein's innovative *Oklahoma!* with his own "integrated" musical score. Anchored by Ethel Merman's brassy performance, *Annie Get Your Gun* was a huge hit; debuting at Broadway's Imperial Theatre on May 16, 1946, it ran on Broadway for 1,147 performances and seemed to assure Berlin's continued preeminence as he entered his fifth decade in show business.

But the show would be his last great success. In October of that same year, M-G-M released *Blue Skies,* which reunited *Holiday Inn*'s dream pairing of Crosby and Astaire but had none of the earlier picture's lightly worn charm. The movie's title announced its complacency: its score leaned heavily on Berlin's catalog, interpolating eighteen old hits, including an inevitable Crosby rehash of "White Christmas." The song-writer's next film, the Astaire-Garland vehicle *Easter Parade* (1948), was a sprightlier affair, featuring six new numbers, two of which, "Steppin' Out with My Baby" and "A Couple of Swells," had some of the boulevardier panache of the classics he'd written for Astaire in the 1930s. But Berlin continued to plunder his songbook's back pages—*Easter Parade*'s best songs were twenty years old.

The songwriter's increasing reliance on old songs told a story of flagging inspiration. New Berlin projects continued to reach the stage and screen with clockwork regularity—in 1949 and 1950 two new musicals, *Miss Liberty* and *Call Me Madam,* opened on Broadway—but by Berlin's standards, they were lead-footed and, tellingly, failed to produce big pop hits. *Miss Liberty,* Berlin's latest exercise in flag-waving—a reflex that was growing tiresome—flopped outright, garnering indifferent reviews and closing after 308 performances. *Call Me Madam* did better at the box office and with critics, but none of its songs made the move from the stage to the Hit Parade.

Berlin's classics, though, continued to haunt American airwaves, and the sturdiest was "White Christmas." Crosby's record returned to the radio every year; and now there were countless new versions by everyone from Nat King Cole to Mantovani, the specialist in orchestral schlock. In fact, the new decade's craze for instrumental "mood music"—Muzak—made the song more inescapable than ever; come December, Berlin's melody was a fixture of the American sonic landscape, piped into elevators and office buildings and department stores. Had he never earned another cent from any other song, "White Christmas" would have been enough to keep Berlin living handsomely. The song's sheet music sales alone were generating more than $300,000 a year.

In 1953, for the first time in the eleven years since it was released, "White Christmas" failed to make the Hit Parade chart. The following year, it returned with a vengeance. In August 1954, a new Berlin film arrived in theaters with a title that promised box office gold: *White Christmas.* For some time, Berlin had been contemplating a project built around his most surefire property; at one point, he had planned to mount a

"White Christmas"–themed Broadway show, a scheme that would have brought the song full circle back to its late 1930s origins. But when Bing Crosby and Fred Astaire agreed to sign on for a *Holiday Inn* retread, Berlin couldn't resist and adapted his story for the screen.

Things did not go smoothly. Astaire disliked the script and begged out. Another song-and-dance man, Donald O'Connor, signed on as Astaire's replacement but fell seriously ill, leaving the production in the lurch. A last-minute pinch hitter, Danny Kaye, was pulled off the Paramount lot, and the filming at last proceeded, with two newcomers, Vera-Ellen and Rosemary Clooney, rounding out the foursome at the center of the movie's rather harebrained love intrigues.

In commercial terms, *White Christmas* was a stupendous success. It was the top box office hit of 1954, grossing more than any previous Berlin film. Its artistic merit was another matter. The film's original songs were forgettable, its gags, flat; with its grating "family entertainment" wholesomeness and garish Technicolor palette, *White Christmas* seems in retrospect supremely and tragically a product of the Eisenhower fifties.

The movie's tackiness was nowhere more apparent than in the handling of its title song. A dozen years after its understated debut in *Holiday Inn,* "White Christmas" is given the Vegas treatment: in the final scene of *White Christmas,* the four leads, trussed up in Santa Claus outfits, sing the number while trimming a tree with a gaggle of eager tots. "White Christmas" kitsch begins here; for the song's reputation as an icon of Christmas schlock—its decades of ill treatment at the hands of

Barbra Streisand, Michael Bolton, and other over-emoters—
Berlin had only himself to blame.

White Christmas's prime accomplishment was to amplify
the legend of its title song and the era that had produced it.
The film is an exercise in wartime nostalgia: its opening scene
finds Crosby singing "White Christmas" to a group of misty,
battle-weary GIs in the bombed ruins of a European city; its
plot revolves around a retired four-star general—as regal as
an American eagle, as lantern-jawed as Ike—and a reunion of
an old army platoon. Less than a decade after VJ day—almost
fifty years before Stephen Ambrose, *The Greatest Generation,* and
Saving Private Ryan—the country was already gazing back
fondly at "the Good War."

Berlin had particular reason to feel wistful about bygone
days: popular culture was changing. In December 1954, while
White Christmas continued its theatrical run, the Drifters, a
five-member rhythm-and-blues vocal ensemble on the upstart
label Atlantic, reached number two on the *Billboard* R&B
charts with a startling reworking of Berlin's Christmas classic.
The Drifters were led by Clyde McPhatter, a handsome
twenty-two-year-old with an astonishing high-tenor voice; the
group had established itself a year earlier with the single
"Money Honey," a number one R&B hit that in future years
was rated by some as the first rock 'n' roll record.

The Drifters' "White Christmas" was just as raw and
exciting as "Money Honey": two minutes, forty seconds of
exuberant doo-wop, delivered over a stark patter of bass and
drums, that was a musical universe away from Crosby's stately
ballad singing. Berlin's only awareness of the Drifters' "White

Christmas" may have been the royalty checks it brought into his New York headquarters (the record was a hit again in 1955 and 1956, this time crossing over to the *Billboard* pop charts). But had Berlin listened to the record, he would have heard an ominous sound. The song's rhythmic dynamism and the erotic urgency of McPhatter's vocal were a herald of things to come: the musical revolution that would knock the songwriter off his throne and bring to a close the pop music era that "White Christmas" had crowned.

Ironically, it was a musical sea change that "White Christmas" had anticipated and helped catalyze. In 1940, at the same time that Berlin was putting the final touches on "White Christmas," a contract dispute arose between national radio stations and the American Society of Composers, Authors and Publishers, the organization Berlin had helped found a generation before to enforce the payment of licensing fees to songwriters. For the year-plus that the two sides fought out the terms of a contract renegotiation, ASCAP's properties—the songs of Berlin, Kern, Gershwin, and nearly every other leading pop songwriter—disappeared from the airwaves. In their place, listeners heard tunes of an older vintage: Stephen Foster, turn-of-the-century parlor ballads, other songs published before the formation of ASCAP. Along with those older popular standards, mainstream radio began playing folk songs, "hillbilly music," the various black styles the record industry lumped together as "race music"—sounds previously aired only on small, regional radio stations.

By the time the ASCAP dispute ended in 1941, Americans had embraced songs like "You Are My Sunshine," and their appetites had been whetted for an earthier sound; Tin Pan Alley began producing folksier fare to meet the demand. The most successful of these offerings, of course, was "White Christmas," whose enormous crossover success—Crosby's record appeared on the pop, country, and rhythm-and-blues charts—foretold the larger musical cross-pollination that would take place in the 1950s and 1960s, when various strains of American vernacular music collapsed into mainstream pop and reformulated as rock 'n' roll.

But there was a more profound sense in which "White Christmas" had paved the way for the new music. For as long as popular music had existed as a mass medium, it had been a composer's game, an industry focused on the production of songs in the form of written scores. Tin Pan Alley was pop music's symbolic epicenter; songwriters were its stars. The Hit Parade chart reflected this emphasis, measuring the sales of sheet music—not records—and the number of times songs appeared on radio broadcasts in different versions. Although performers played a pivotal role in promoting songs, composers strove to create durable standards that would transcend any one performance and took pains to write androgynous lyrics, suitable for male or female singers.

When Crosby's recording carried "White Christmas" to American troops and to record-shattering sales, it crystallized a music-industry transformation that had been gathering force for the two decades since the advent of phonograph records and big-time radio: the shift from an emphasis on the sale of sheet music scores to records—from the songs themselves to performances by singing charismatics. Crosby's record had broken "White Christmas," and though Berlin gloried in the song's continued sheet music profits, it was the royalties from Crosby's recording that really brought in the big bucks. Crosby's "White Christmas" marked the commercial pinnacle of the song standard era, but it also foretold its demise. Tin Pan Alley was being left behind; the musical future belonged to singers.

The new supremacy of the performer was dramatized by the emergence of Elvis Presley. In 1956, Presley roared from Memphis onto the charts with his exhilarating mix of rockabilly and rhythm and blues. Tin Pan Alley had sniffed at rock 'n' roll, dismissing it as a fleeting craze, but Presley's astronomical record sales told a different story. The singles "Hound Dog" and "I Want You, I Need You" each sold more than 1 million copies; the sales orders for "Love Me Tender" were more than a million even before the record arrived in stores. "Hound Dog"/"Don't Be Cruel" sold more than 3 million in a year—a mark it had taken Crosby's "White Christmas" years to reach—and topped the pop, country, and R&B charts simultaneously. In all, Presley sold more than 10 million records in 1956. These astonishing numbers proclaimed the arrival of a new group of record buyers: teenagers. The bobbysox mania that greeted Frank Sinatra's Paramount performances in the previous decade looked like Junior League gatherings next to the youth hysteria ignited by Presley's thrilling songs and swiveling hips.

The reaction to Presley replayed the ragtime culture wars of the turn of the century. Again, cries of alarm came not just from moralists and the clergy but from the musical establishment; this time, though, the foes of the new music weren't guardians of "high" classical music culture but Tin Pan Alley's leading lights, who scorned rock 'n' roll as devoid of melody and sex-obsessed—charges that should have had a familiar ring to Berlin, the erstwhile ragtime king. With their Hit Parade eminence suddenly under siege, the old guard's rhetoric became shrill. "Rock 'n' roll smells phony and false," Sinatra said at the height of the Presley craze. "It is sung, played, and written for the most part by cretinous goons and by means of its almost imbecilic reiteration, and sly, lewd, in plain fact, dirty lyrics it manages to be the martial music of every sideburned delinquent on the face of the earth. It is the most brutal, ugly, desperate, vicious form of expression it has been my misfortune to hear."

In November 1957, a new LP arrived on record-store shelves with a cover photo of Presley, dewy-eyed beneath a glistening hillock of pomaded hair, gazing across a snow-blanketed landscape. *Elvis' Christmas Album,* the first major rock 'n' roll Christmas LP, featured a dozen tunes, ranging from modern Christmas classics ("I'll Be Home for Christmas") to traditional hymns ("Silent Night," "O Little Town of Bethlehem") to double-entendre-packed blues ("Santa Claus Is Back in Town"). The album was greeted by hoots from the usual suspects, outraged at what was regarded as Presley's rock 'n' roll desecration of the traditional Christmas.

The most prominent voice in that anti-Presley concord belonged to Irving Berlin. Although the album's big hit was a remake of the Ernest Tubb country standard "Blue Christmas," its cause célèbre was Presley's "White Christmas," a bravura gloss on the Drifters' arrangement of the tune. Indignant at Presley's cavalier treatment of his most famous song, the songwriter instructed his staff to telephone radio stations around the country demanding a ban on the record.

In hindsight, it's hard not to view this clash—pitting the cantankerous Tin Pan Alley tycoon against the ascendant "king" of rock 'n' roll—as a parable marking the passing of the musical zeitgeist. But if Berlin epitomized his musical generation's belligerence about the new music, he was right to suspect that Presley was having a bit too much fun with his Christmas song. It is an especially hammy performance, filled with all sorts of raffish Elvisisms: Presley slurs and swallows phrases, elongates the word *children* into five rumbling syllables (*cha-hil-dra-heh-hen*), moves dramatically from his feathery upper register to his trademark boudoir basso and back again. Given his sensitive renditions of "I'll Be Home for Christmas," "Silent Night," and the album's other seasonal sacred cows, one can't help but hear some mischief-making in Presley's "White Christmas." It is a musical slingshot aimed not at Berlin but at the "owner" of this song, the older generation's singing superstar—"Santa Cros" himself. Presley even includes his own tremulous take on a Crosby mordent on the word *dreaming*.

Berlin's anti-Presley crusade saw some minor victories. In Los Angeles, a popular disc jockey refused to air Presley's "White Christmas," telling listeners that doing so would be akin to allowing the stripper Tempest Storm to "give Christmas gifts to my kids." In Portland, Oregon, radio station KEX ordered the record stricken from its playlist on the grounds that Presley's "treatment of the song was in very poor taste"; when one station DJ played the tune, he was promptly fired.

But ultimately, Berlin's was a doomed battle. Although most Canadian broadcasters banned *Elvis' Christmas Album*, when CKWS in Kingston, Ontario, solicited listeners' opinions on the controversy, 93 percent of the eight hundred respondents endorsed the record. Americans agreed: just three weeks after it was released, *Elvis' Christmas Album* claimed the top spot on *Billboard*'s Pop LPs chart, where it stayed for the duration of the Christmas season. Flipping the radio dial that December, you were as likely to hear Presley's "White Christmas" as Crosby's—a fact Berlin couldn't have failed to recognize as a sign of his diminished clout. The mob had spoken; for the first time in a half century, Berlin found himself on the wrong side of popular taste.

Berlin's growing alienation from the mob took a toll on his spirits. As the hits dwindled, Berlin's old anxieties resurfaced: he fretted that his talent had abandoned him, struggled with bouts of paralyzing depression, suffered panic attacks in the presence of colleagues and collaborators. In 1953, Crosby came to the songwriter's home to hear him demonstrate the new songs he had written for the upcoming *White Christmas* film. Berlin was overcome with fear in the company of the great singer; he couldn't play the songs, or even really speak. "Do you like the songs, Irving?" Crosby asked. Berlin nodded. "Then they're good enough for me," Crosby said.

As the 1950s progressed, Berlin's output dropped off. In 1958, for the first time in a half century, Berlin did not copyright a new song. He took up hobbies—he had developed a new passion for painting—but he felt himself "heading for a breakdown." Finally, exhausted, racked by insomnia and frayed nerves, he checked himself into a hospital, where he was treated for severe depression. When he returned home, Irving Berlin announced his retirement. It was 1959; he had thirty more years to live.

Three difficult years later, after several subsequent hospitalizations, Berlin decided to return to songwriting. "I looked at myself and said, 'What you need is to go back to work,'" Berlin recalled. "It was wonderful. I threw out the medicines, paid off the doctors, and sat down and did what for almost sixty years I have done best. . . . My spirits soared." Berlin felt reconnected to his muse; what's more, he was at work on what seemed a can't-miss "angle": a new musical about a young president and first lady modeled on the current White House residents, the Kennedys.

But a career resurrection was not in the cards. Beginning with a disastrous gala opening attended by the Kennedys at the National Theater in Washington, *Mr. President* was the most ill-starred of all Berlin productions. New York critics savaged the show. The *Herald Tribune* scolded Berlin for a ham-handed score that ignored "all the old-fashioned rules for songwriting"; the *Journal-American* chided Berlin's patriotic songs for giving "corn a bad name"; *Time* magazine compared *Mr. President* to the *Titanic* and declared it the "worst musical on Broadway."

Berlin's failure was one not just of execution but conception. With *Mr. President*'s tribute to the glamorous first couple, Berlin had tried to once again capture the zeitgeist; but fawning over the president, he proved himself out of touch with the mood of the dawning decade, an era in which protest music would migrate from the folk fringe to the mainstream, when pop songs would give voice to blistering antiestablishment grievances, and even the most apolitical tunes seemed charged with the mischievous *épater le bourgeois* energy of the counterculture.

The 1960s proved decisive in bringing an end to the musical age that Berlin had dominated. In the early part of the decade, classic pop vied with rock 'n' roll for chart preeminence. Sinatra's brilliant string of Capitol Records albums in the 1950s and early 1960s breathed new life into old standards and minted new ones. But few other torch carriers of the old tradition had Sinatra's charisma and interpretive insight; and in 1963, even Sinatra was reckoning with rock 'n' roll, recording songs like "Softly, As I Leave You," whose steady backbeat was a gawky concession to the new sound.

By the time of the Beatles' appearance on the *Ed Sullivan Show* in February of 1964—an event that registered as the dawn-of-a-new-age thunderclap, coming fast in the aftermath of President Kennedy's assassination—rock 'n' roll's conquest was complete. Popular music decentralized, breaking free of New York's stranglehold; the Broadway musical, which in the heyday of song standards supplied so much of the nation's dance music and ballad hits, became boutique entertainment, aimed at an older audience, estranged from populist sound that had captivated the nation's youth. The pop mainstream was invigorated by the arrival of new voices from the cultural margins, in particular those of African-Americans. Volume was boosted; rhythm claimed primacy over melody. For a while, the songwriters of the Brill Building and the Motown Hit Factory carried forward a modern variation on the Tin Pan Alley songwriting tradition, but Bob Dylan and the Beatles soon paved the way for the rise of singer-songwriters—the "unprofessionals," as Berlin and other old-timers churlishly called them.

Berlin and company were right to think that their heyday represented a musical Golden Age of a certain sort. Broadway and Hollywood songwriters prized craft above all, and their best efforts had a Fabergé Egg delicacy that has not been replicated in the rock era. In "My Funny Valentine," in "Someone to Watch Over Me," in "White Christmas," we find a combination of charm, craftsmanship, and feeling unique in American popular music.

But the rock era didn't bring lesser pleasures, just different ones. And though the old-timers have maligned rock-era music as kids's stuff—and, like Fred Astaire, huffed at its "nudie rudie" licentiousness—it was in many ways more mature than the songs of the Golden Age. It was music for a different world, less steeped in the moon-June mythologies and dreams of consensus that the avid assimilators behind the American Songbook had held so dear. The rock 'n' roll revolution was preeminently about a new kind of freedom—freedom that was inscribed not just in the music's raised volume and driving rhythms but in the opening up of popular song to a greater number of voices and viewpoints. Listening to songwriters from Bob Dylan to James Brown, from the Beatles to Marvin Gaye to Joni Mitchell, we can't help but feel the excitement of popular song's liberation from Tin Pan Alley's hegemony. Golden Age songwriters were the first to make poetry out of pop lyrics; but rock and soul songwriters, taking their cues from the gritty testimonials of the blues, said that pop-song content could be as varied and unblushing as literature. In any case, by the mid-1960s, Berlin knew his professional time was up. "It was as if I owned a store and people no longer wanted to buy what I had to sell," he recalled. "It was time to close up shop."

Berlin, who lived so much of his life in the glare of klieg lights, was rarely glimpsed during his last quarter century. In May 1973, he surfaced at a gala White House dinner honoring Vietnam War POWs. At the end of the evening, Berlin—at eighty-five years old a hunched, tiny figure—took to the stage. With President Nixon at his side, he led a "God Bless America" sing-along, punching the air with clenched fists—a performance that couldn't have been terribly different from the way he had delivered tearjerkers like "The Mansion of Aching Hearts" and "Bird in a Gilded Cage" as a teenage song busker seventy years earlier. It was his swan song as a performer. He lived another decade and a half but never again made an official public appearance.

Berlin's cranky reputation was well known, and the legends that swirled around his final years depicted a livid, thin-skinned old man, stalking the gloomy rooms of his East Side mansion: the Hermit of Beekman Place. It was said that the songwriter poured wrath on those who approached him with requests for copyright permission, that the greetings of strangers who encountered Berlin on his rare outings were met with imperious silence or tart tongue-lashings.

The elderly Berlin was a grump. But he was also a doting grandfather and passionate amateur painter. His attention to his business affairs never flagged; he called his office every day to check in and scolded fellow senior citizen Helmy Kresa when he discovered that Kresa had left work early on a Friday. Berlin kept in touch with old friends like Ira Gershwin and Harold Arlen by phone and in witty letters that, frequently, took the form of light verse. "Seventy-one / Can be fun," he wrote to Arlen on his birthday. "If you still have bullets / In your gun."

And although most people assumed that he had long since stopped, he continued to write songs. Once in a rare while, he would pick up the phone, call his office, and have his secretary Hilda Schneider take down a new lyric, or rarer still, have Kresa transcribe a new composition. As he confided to a friend, "As long as I'm able, whether the songs are good or bad, I'll continue to write them because songwriting is not just a business with me. It's everything."

Berlin's last songs were, for the most part, simply lyrics, typed by the songwriter in hunt-and-peck fashion on green steno-notebook paper. For fifty years he had had the nation's ear; now, for the first time, Berlin was writing songs for Berlin alone. Some of the songs were topical; we have Berlin on Watergate and its aftermath ("They Can't Pick on Dick Anymore"; "Carter and Mondale"), and Berlin on the Soviet Union ("Alexander Solzhenitsyn"). But the most moving of these last compositions find a lion-in-winter Berlin grappling with solitude and old age, with the deaths of friends, with his past glories and his professional oblivion in the rock era. Their titles are telling: "If You Didn't Know How Old You Were," "Old Men," "Growing Gray." One of the songwriter's last creations was written in February of 1987, when he was ninety-eight years old, two and half years before his death at the age of one hundred and one. Its title: "Old Songs."

> *Old songs bring back the old days,*
> *The golden old days when we were young.*
> *Simple songs that we sang then*
> *Keep reminding us to sing them again.*
> *With old friends we'll sing the old songs,*
> *Bring back the old days gone by.*
> *There will always be old songs,*
> *Because old songs never die.*

Irving Berlin was a decade and a half Bing Crosby's senior; the songwriter outlived the singer by twelve years. During the final decade of Crosby's life, Berlin had long since retreated from public view. Crosby, meanwhile, was enjoying a sunnier semiretirement, recording and performing occasionally, golfing or going to the horse races almost daily.

Yet the old crooner hadn't entirely ceded the spotlight. He returned to public prominence every December in the role that Berlin's most famous "old song" had secured for him: "The Voice of Christmas." *Holiday Inn* and *White Christmas* were fixtures of holiday season late-late shows. But Crosby's big annual star-turn was his Christmas television special, a latter-day variation on the *Kraft Music Hall* Christmas radio broadcasts. The first of these specials aired in 1961 on NBC TV; they immediately established themselves as a rite of the nation's annual Christmas season. The nostalgia that surrounded the Christmas holiday not only stirred longings for the Victorian Christmas that "White Christmas" depicted, but, in the age of rock 'n' roll, inspired a yearning to revisit the popular culture of an earlier, seemingly more genteel and felicitous era. So it was that millions of Americans tuned in every year to witness a comforting yuletide tableau: Crosby singing holiday standards, flanked by his second wife, Kathryn, and their children, Harry, Nathaniel, and Mary Frances, Christmas lights twinkling on an evergreen behind him.

These programs were not in the greatest taste. The production values were slapdash, the between-song banter insipid, the baubles a bit too garishly bright. There was something a bit depressing about the C-list celebrity guest stars who turned up on the broadcasts—Robert Goulet, Mac Davis, Sally Struthers. And though the presence of Bing's children struck the seasonally correct family-values note, they couldn't really carry a tune, and as the years passed and their hair got shaggier, it seemed obvious that they would rather have been at a Foghat concert than in front of a hearth fire singing "Deck the Halls" with dear old dad.

Yet when Crosby sang, he managed to transcend the tawdriness of the spectacle and its shopworn sentimentality. Even the occasional awkward nod to rock 'n' roll didn't quite snap the spell. On Crosby's final Christmas special in 1977, David Bowie turned up for an intergenerational summit. With Bowie dressed for the occasion—in a stockbroker-sober navy blue suit, with a gold crucifix dangling from his necklace—the pair gave a touchingly maladroit duet of "The Little Drummer Boy" and "Peace on Earth." But the highlight of Crosby's Christmas broadcasts was always its wistful finale: "White Christmas."

Today, Berlin's song remains a paradox: both the saddest and most beloved of all Christmas songs. Indeed, the melancholy quality of "White Christmas" may well account for its continued preeminence. Better than any other Christmas carol, "White Christmas" captures the ambivalent feelings that we bring to the holiday. Song after song insists that the season is a time of unmitigated joy and merriment; but we know better. Who hasn't had the holiday blues?

Christmas is, among other things, our most reliable annual anticlimax. Every year, the Christmas season seduces us with an ideal we are doomed never to attain. December arrives, and we are clobbered by images promising a magical return to a state of grace, a perfect holiday of merry and bright days and silent nights—so we keep shopping. Yet the very forces that stir hopes for an ideal Christmas—the bombardment of television commercials and the happy clamor of yuletide tunes—seem to frustrate our ability to experience it. While we guide a shopping cart piled with video games into the checkout aisle, how can we help but be caught short when we hear the melancholy sound of Bing Crosby, singing that hopeful, sad benediction: "May your days be merry and bright / And may all your Christmases be white"? The power of "White Christmas" is its ambivalence: it depicts both the mythic ideal of Christmas—the cottage home, the children, the snowfall—and the inevitable letdown, the bummer of holiday dreams unfulfilled. Deep down, we know that ambivalence is closer to the real Christmas experience than the cheer we hear in a hundred blither, lesser songs.

Irving Berlin and Bing Crosby were never the closest of friends. Yet they had a special bond, born of professional respect and a sense of their shared achievements. "Ours has been, I think, a very close relationship without much emotion passing between us," Berlin told Crosby in a 1953 letter.

The touchstone of that relationship was the song that was their first and greatest collaboration. During the final years of Crosby's life, the singer and songwriter traded annual Christmas letters, focusing, invariably, on "White Christmas," which Berlin, in a gesture he made to no other collaborator, referred to as "our song." "I see the picture 'White Christmas' is getting considerable exposure this season," Crosby wrote to Berlin in 1964. "Of course, I'll be eternally grateful to you for that wonderful song and all it's done for me."

The following December, the songwriter Jimmy Van Heusen showed up at the Hollywood Palace, where Crosby was rehearsing his Christmas broadcast, bearing a portrait that Berlin had painted of the singer. "I painted this about two years ago and, frankly, had no idea when I started that it would turn out to resemble you," Berlin wrote.

I was reluctant to send it on until Jimmy Van Heusen saw it one night last week and told me that you would get a kick out of it. Please don't feel that you have to hang it up. As a painter, I'm still a pretty good song-writer. But regardless of its merit as a painting, I intend it to be a token of my affectionate regard for the guy who is so much a part of my most successful song. I will never forget your remark after I first played and sang it for you at the Paramount Studio—"You don't have to worry about this one, Irving." How right you were. May all yours be white.

Two years later, Berlin wrote Crosby again. "It's a little late—after almost twenty-seven years—to send you a fan let-ter about 'White Christmas,' but I heard you sing it last night on the Hollywood Palace show and not alone were you the first, but you remain the best," Berlin wrote.

"I never cease to reflect what a lucky break it was for me when I wound up with 'White Christmas' in 'Holiday Inn,'" Crosby replied.

In December 1976, Crosby arrived in New York for a series of benefit concerts. His Christmas show had aired on CBS on December 1. On December 6, he performed a benefit for the Fordham Prep School at Avery Fisher Hall, his first concert date in New York in several years. The next night, Crosby and his family began a two-week stand at the Uris Theatre on Broadway. On the fifteenth, a throng gathered at City Hall to watch the annual lighting of the city's Christmas tree. In a surprise, Crosby appeared on the City Hall steps. While the lights on the tree flickered to life, the seventy-three-year-old singer, in baritone voice that had lost little of its mellow luster, eased into the chorus of "White Christmas."

That evening, Irving Berlin was seventy-five blocks north of City Hall, in his Beekman Place mansion. A week earlier, before the first of Crosby's Broadway concerts, Berlin had wired the singer at the Uris Theatre. There was a mischievous hint of old Tin Pan Alley in the note, the last that the pair would exchange: at age eighty-eight, Berlin was still a song-plugger.

DEAR BING: GOOD LUCK TONIGHT TO YOU AND YOUR FAMILY. IF YOU'RE STUCK FOR A FINISH I'VE GOT A SONG ABOUT CHRISTMAS THAT I WROTE SOME YEARS AGO THAT YOU MIGHT CONSIDER. LOVE.

IRVING

Acknowledgments

✦

This book is the result of many kindnesses; to properly acknowledge all of them would take another book. I'll do my best to say thanks in a few paragraphs.

My first and greatest debt is to the Berlin family, in particular Mary Ellin Barrett and Linda Emmet, whose generosity made this project possible. They enthusiastically supported my work, facilitated my access to their father's papers at the Library of Congress, cheerfully answered my (often inane) questions, read my manuscript, and helped make sure I had my facts straight. They did all this without for one minute trying to influence my interpretation of events or in any way encroaching on what might rather grandly be called my scholarly independence. I am especially grateful to Mary Ellin Barrett for her warmth and encouragement, for allowing me to read her father's correspondence at her kitchen table, and for her own book, *Irving Berlin: A Daughter's Memoir*—a trove of Berlinania and a model of graceful prose writing to which I turned again and again for information and inspiration.

I wish to thank Bert Fink of the Irving Berlin Music Company, for his invaluable help at all stages of this project and for tolerating my rambling voice mail messages. Thanks also to Flora Griggs and Robin Walton of the Irving Berlin Music Company.

White Christmas would not have been possible were it not for many very busy people who gave me their time; answered my cold calls; offered advice, recollections, and expertise; and in other ways aided my research and helped shape my thinking. I am indebted to: Gary Giddins, Robert Kimball, Jackson Lears, Deborah Dash Moore, Karal Ann Manning, David Nasaw, John Klier, Stephen Holden, Marilyn Plotkins, Max Wilk, Walter Wager, Philip Furia, Ed Jablonski, Ken Emerson, Paul Charosh, Will Friedwald, Steven Lasker, Miles Kruger, Ridge Walker, Walter Scharf, and Alan Scharf. Many thanks to Amy Asch for sharing her vast knowledge of Berlin's papers and her insights about "White Christmas." Thanks to Ray White at the Library of Congress for making my research such a pleasure. I am grateful for the help of two distinguished music scholars, Charles Hamm and Jefferey Magee, for taking the time to answer my questions and for writing the best things ever published on Irving Berlin.

Hamilton Cain convinced me that my idea for a book on "White Christmas" wasn't harebrained. He also helped me through the difficult early stages of writing my book proposal. I thank him.

Thanks to my wonderful agent, Bill Clegg, for his friendship, tireless work on my behalf, great career advice, editorial intelligence, and impeccably timed pep talks.

I owe particular thanks to Gillian Blake, my editor at Scribner. She saw this book through many difficult moments, tolerated a scandalous number of missed deadlines, and was in every way an ideal editor for this first-time author. Thanks also to Gillian's assistant Rachel Sussman and, of course, to Nan Graham and the rest of the team at Scribner.

I wish to thank a number of friends and family members: Jacob Gould Rosen, Roslyn Rosen Lund, Van Metre Lund, Sarah Bowles, Cheryl Gould, Roberta Stone, Dylan Pringle, John Slover, Jon Seder, Stephen Lynch, Eric Colburn, Doug Berkson, Robert Mackey, Julie Weiss, Cassandra Lozano, Mason Rader, Orbit Lozano-Rader, Daniel Adams, Betsy Seder, Emma Taylor, Mia Hatgis, Frederick Witherspoon, Ishée, Louis Lowe, Ian LeBon, and Ned J. Soyor. Thanks also to the staff at Doma Café and, as always, big up the Chez Brigitte Massive.

I am especially grateful for the friendship of Philip Nobel, by the far the best writer I know, who made many excellent suggestions about the manuscript.

My grandmother Midge Grant introduced me to the recordings of Frank Sinatra and Ella Fitzgerald when I was a kid and inspired my interest in song standards. I've always associated the charm of those old songs with her, and never would have written this book without her. Thanks, Grandma.

Gillian Kane made me swear I wouldn't dedicate this book to her; if I ever write another one, I can't make the same promise. She kept me sane and happy and was my inspiration during the year I wrote *White Christmas*. I hope some of her wit rubbed off on me and made it into the book.

White Christmas is dedicated to my parents, Susan Grant Rosen and Marc Rosen, whose love and support I can never repay. If there is any clear thinking about history and culture in these pages, it is the result of conversations with my mother, a great scholar with a prose style I would kill for. I love her, and I love my Dad, and I hope they like this book.

Notes

✦

3 God gave Moses: Philip Roth, *Operation Shylock: A Confession* (New York: Simon & Schuster, 1993), p. 157.

3 They say a hanging man: Kurt Vonnegut, *Mother Night* (New York: Delta, 1999) (reprint), p. 288.

4 He strove to write: *Boston American*, October 4, 1954.

5 Alec Wilder, in his landmark study: Alec Wilder, *American Popular Song: The Great Innovators, 1900–1954* (New York: Oxford University Press, 1990).

6 in a knowing nod to its creator's pedigree, Yiddish: The Yiddish version was recorded by Mandy Patinkin, as "Der Alter Tzigayner/White Christmas," on *Mamaloshen* (Nonesuch/Atlantic, 1998).

6 Sales of "White Christmas": Statistics courtesy of the Irving Berlin Music Company.

8 "just beneath the surface . . .": Laurence Bergreen, *As Thousands Cheer: The Life of Irving Berlin* (New York: Penguin Books, 1990), p. 410.

9 a "Why We Fight" song: H. Mark Glancy, "Dreaming of Christmas: Hollywood and the Second World War," in Mark

Connelly, ed., *Christmas at the Movies* (London: I. B. Tauris, 2000), p. 65.

10 what historian Ann Douglas has called: Ann Douglas, *Terrible Honesty: Mongrel Manhattan in the 1920s* (New York: Farrar, Straus and Giroux, 1995).

17 "White Christmas" enters the written record: The first manuscript copy of "White Christmas," dated January 8, 1940, is housed in the Irving Berlin Collection of the Music Division of the Library of Congress (IBC-LC).

18 He told his friend Miles Kruger: Author interview with Miles Kruger.

18 The *Los Angeles Mirror* reported: *Los Angeles Mirror,* December 21, 1954.

18 In an "exclusive interview" with *The American Weekly*: *American Weekly,* December 19, 1954.

18 "When I wrote 'White Christmas' in 1941": *Philadelphia Inquirer,* October 10, 1954.

18 According to Kresa: Bergreen, *As Thousands Cheer*, pp. 386–87. Bergreen's account of Berlin's arrival at his office with "White Christmas" is based on his interview with the late Helmy Kresa. My own research in Berlin's papers at the Library of Congress confirms aspects of Bergreen's account. The date of the first "White Christmas" lead sheet, in Kresa's handwriting, *does* agree with his contention that Berlin showed up with the song on a Monday morning; and I have accepted as accurate the quotations Bergreen attributes to Berlin per Kresa's recollections. It must be noted, however, that other parts of Bergreen's "White Christmas" story are patent fiction. He breathlessly narrates Berlin's writing of the song in an all-night session—an event he can't be sure ever actually took place. This kind of invention is typical of Bergreen's rather slipshod method, and while I accept the quotations and recollections he credits to Kresa, there is a great deal to be skeptical of in his biography.

19 "He's a buzz saw": *Detroit Free Press,* December 26, 1942.

19 When Queen Elizabeth: Edward Jablonski, *Irving Berlin: American Troubadour* (New York: Henry Holt and Company, 1999), p. 222.

19 In 1912: Philip Furia, *Irving Berlin: A Life in Song* (New York: Schirmer Books, 1998), p. 54.

20 All told, Berlin wrote: Ibid., p. 2.

20 *He wakes her up and cries*: "I've Written Another Song" in IBC-LC.

21 "if I had not so much admiration": Letter from Helmy Kresa to Abraham L. Berman, September 1964, IBC-LC.

22 "The melody doesn't come to you": *Boston American,* October 4, 1954.

23 His trademark feature: Mary Ellin Barrett, *Irving Berlin: A Daughter's Memoir* (New York: Simon & Schuster, 1994), p. 16.

23 "I want you to take down a song": Bergreen, *As Thousands Cheer*, p. 386.

27 Christmas has woven a pattern: *American Weekly,* December 19, 1954.

27 Mel Tormé's 1992 recording: The song appears on Mel Tormé, *Christmas Songs* (Telarc, 1992).

28 "is hardly ever used": Undated note from IB to Rosemary Clooney, IBC-LC.

30 "You make all the rest of us": Letter from Jerome Kern to IB, July 16, 1942, IBC-LC.

30 Berlin's notes for *The Music Box Revue of 1938*: *Music Box Revue of 1939* subject file in IBC-LC.

31 *It's in three acts:* Ibid.

31 Act one—"The Present." 1939: Ibid.

33 First-act closers emphasized production values: Author conversation with Marilyn Plotkins.

34 an error Berlin shrugged off: Barrett, *Daughter's Memoir,* p. 178.

34 According to biographer Philip Furia: Furia, *Life in Song,* p. 202.

34 He began making notes: The quotes that follow are from the *Music Box Revue of 1939* subject file in IBC-LC.

35 "He just couldn't bring himself": Author interview with Mary Ellin Barrett.

35 "There's no Lindy's in Los Angeles": Jablonski, *Troubadour,* p. 196.

35 a shiksa wife: Berlin's 1926 marriage to Ellin Mackay, the Catholic daughter of *New York Telegraph* magnate Clarence Mackay, may have been the most famous intermarriage of the 1920s. The couple eloped, over the objections of the bride's father, an event that made national headlines and scandalized New York society. For many observers, the Berlin-Mackay marriage caught the anything-goes spirit of the Jazz age, with its Turkey Trotting flappers, rising hemlines, and crumbling old guard.

35 here, a Passover seder: For more on Berlin's agnosticism see Barrett, *Daughter's Memoir*, pp. 122–24.

35 "the single most beautiful and exciting day": Ibid., pp. 124–28.

36 "seemed to tower to Heaven": *American Weekly*, December 19, 1954.

36 which scraped the ceiling: Barrett, *Daughter's Memoir*, p. 125.

36 BERLINS' INFANT SON DIES OF HEART ATTACK: *New York Times*, December 26, 1928.

37 Mary Ellin herself only learned: Barrett, *Daughter's Memoir*, pp. 59–60.

37 "went somewhere": Ibid., p. 60.

37 "We both hated Christmas": Ibid., p. 127.

37 bought the first sheet music copy: Robert Kimball and Linda Emmet, *The Complete Lyrics of Irving Berlin* (New York: Knopf, 2001), p. 4.

37 "You said one very wise": Letter from IB to Joseph Schenck, April 18, 1956.

44 the lyrics of Ira Gershwin: For an excellent discussion of golden age lyric writing, see Philip Furia, *The Poets of Tin Pan Alley: A History of America's Great Lyricists* (New York: Oxford University Press, 1990).

45 "Blah, blah, blah, blah love": George and Ira Gershwin, "Blah, Blah, Blah" (1931).

46 "world" of two: Richard Crawford, *America's Musical Life* (New York: W. W. Norton, 2001), p. 673.

46 "Millions of people go by": Al Dubin and Harry Warren, "I Only Have Eyes for You" (1934).

47 per capita personal income was $474 per year: U.S. Depart-

ment of Commerce, Bureau of Economic Analysis, *Survey of Current Business.* Found on internet at: http://www.bea.doc.gov/bea/regional/spi/

48 demise of Broadway and Hollywood's songwriting elite: Furia, *Life in Song,* p. 189.

48 "as high as an elephant's eye": "Oh, What a Beautiful Mornin'" (1943).

50 On the journey back to New York: Kimball and Emmet, *Complete Lyrics,* pp. 321–22.

51 tension between progress and nostalgia: Lawrence Levine, *The Unpredictable Past: Explorations in American Cultural History* (New York: Oxford University Press, 1993), pp. 189–230; Warren I. Susman, *Culture as History: The Transformation of American Society in the Twentieth Century* (New York: Pantheon Books, 1973), pp. 150–83.

51 The census revealed that America was now an urban nation: Douglas, *Terrible Honesty,* p. 4.

51 The increased cultural and political stature of cities: Levine, *Unpredictable Past,* p. 195.

51 provided by ancestral and communal ties: Crawford, *America's Musical Life,* p. 674.

52 "someone to watch over me": George and Ira Gershwin, "Someone to Watch over Me" (1926).

52 "In the roaring traffic's boom": Cole Porter, "Night and Day" (1932).

52 Depictions of small-town simplicity: Susman, *Culture as History,* pp. 205–7; Jackson Lears, *Fables of Abundance: A Cultural History of Advertising in America* (New York: Basic Books, 1994), pp. 383–86, *passim.*

52 the Truly American . . . the "American way of life": Susman, *Culture as History.*

53 ideology of the folk revival: Robert Cantwell, *When We Were Good: The Folk Revival* (Cambridge: Harvard University Press, 1996); Benjamin Filene, *Romancing the Folk: Public Memory and American Roots Music* (Chapel Hill: The University of North Carolina Press, 2000).

53 "sissy-voiced" crooners: Robert Christgau, "Woody Guthrie's Second Life," *Village Voice*, June 6, 2000.

54 The New York World's Fair: Geoffrey Perrett, *Days of Sadness, Years of Triumph: The American People, 1939–1945* (Madison: University of Wisconsin Press, 1973), p. 129; Susman, *Culture as History*, pp. 211–29.

55 "When he sang the chorus": Bergreen, *As Thousands Cheer*, p. 386.

55 "played so often": Wilder, *American Popular Song*, p. 94.

56 "a window with no snow beyond it": Mark W. Booth, *The Experience of Songs* (New Haven, Conn.: Yale University Press, 1981), pp. 189–90.

57 Michael Beckerman has pointed out: *New York Times*, December 20, 1998.

61 While in Washington, D.C: *Holiday Inn* subject file, IBC-LC.

62 "There is already one song": Letter from IB to George Cohen on September 3, 1940, IBC-LC.

66 "the epicenter of American Jewish culture": Stephen J. Whitfield, *In Search of American Jewish Culture* (Hanover, N.H.: Brandeis University Press, 1999), p. 61.

66 Tin Pan Alley's "good Jewish music"?: For an erudite discussion of this topic—and one of the finest pieces of Irving Berlin scholarship—see Jeffrey Magee, "Irving Berlin's 'Blue Skies': Ethnic Affiliations and Musical Transformations," in *Musical Quarterly*, Winter 2000, pp. 537–80. Also see Jeffrey Melnick, *A Right to Sing the Blues: African Americans, Jews and American Popular Song* (Cambridge: Harvard University Press, 1999); Charles Hamm, *Irving Berlin: Songs from the Melting Pot: The Formative Years, 1907–1914* (New York: Oxford University Press, 1997); and Michael Alexander, *Jazz Age Jews* (Princeton, N.J.: Princeton University Press, 2001).

67 "a commercialized Wailing Wall": Magee, "Blue Skies," p. 539.

67 "transmuted into music": Alexander Woollcott, *The Story of Irving Berlin* (New York: Da Capo, 1983), p. 30. Woollcott's book, the first Berlin biography, was originally published in 1925, when its subject was thirty-seven years old.

67 "not a single element": Abraham Z. Idelsohn, *Jewish Music: Its Historical Development* (New York: Dover, 1992), p. 474.

67 "hogwash": Jerry Leiber and Mike Stoller, letter published in the *New York Times*, September 9, 2001.

69 Berlin was asked how: *American Weekly,* December 19, 1954.

69 The "Jewboy who named himself": Gary Giddins, *Visions of Jazz* (New York: Oxford University Press, 1998), p. 33.

70 eight Balines: There would have been nine residents of 330 Cherry Street had one of Izzy's sisters not moved in with her young husband.

71 "he just dreams and sings to himself": Bergreen, *As Thousands Cheer,* p. 12.

71 "Everyone should have a Lower East Side in their lives": Ibid., p. 8.

71 "Had I been born on the Lower East Side": Max Wilk, *They're Playing Our Song: Conversations with America's Classic Songwriters* (New York: Da Capo, 1997), p. 170.

72 On Lower East Side street corners: For an excellent discussion of the musical culture of the Lower East Side, see Mark Slobin, *Tenement Songs: The Popular Music of Jewish Immigrants* (Chicago: University of Illinois Press, 1982).

74 songs about America and the immigrant experience: Ibid.

74 "The whole neighborhood is teeming": Konrad Cercovici, *Around the World in New York* (New York: Century Company, 1924), p. 86.

75 Jewish parents, he recalled: Wilk, *They're Playing,* p. 42.

75 Sammy Cahn was more succinct: Ibid., p. 169.

75 The favorite instrument . . . was the piano: Andrew R. Heinze, *Adapting to Abundance: Jewish Immigrants, Mass Consumption and the Search for American Identity* (New York: Columbia University Press, 1990), pp. 133–44; Craig H. Roell, *The Piano in America, 1890–1940* (Chapel Hill: University of North Carolina Press, 1989).

76 Sophie Tucker: Sophie Tucker, *Some of These Days: The Autobiography of Sophie Tucker* (Garden City, N.Y.: Doubleday, 1945).

76 A $5 used piano: Interview with Irving Caesar, *Columbia Universty Oral History Project, Series I, Volume 1, Part 1.*

76 Harry Ruby remembers: Wilk, *They're Playing,* p. 42.

79 the Bucket of Blood, Suicide Hall: Furia, *Life in Song,* p. 13.

80 Old-guard publishing companies: Crawford, *America's Musical Life,* p. 479.

82 (only 33¢): Kimball and Emmet, *Complete Lyrics,* p. 4.

83 "Syncopation is the soul": Andre Millard, *America on Record: A History of Recorded Sound* (New York: Cambridge University Press, 1995), p. 108.

84 "Ragtime is mainly responsible": *Music Trade Review,* October 14, 1911.

90 Jews "became white": See Matthew Frye Jacobson, *Whiteness of a Different Color: European Immigrants and the Alchemy of Race* (Cambridge: Harvard University Press, 1998).

90 Jeffrey Melnick has argued: Melnick, *Right to Sing,* pp. 65–66.

95 "I am not willing": Letter from IB to George Cohen, Jan. 14, 1941, IBC-LC.

95 "a semiclassical": Gary Giddins, *Bing Crosby: A Pocketful of Dreams—The Early Years, 1903–1940* (Boston: Little, Brown, 2001), p. 376.

95 "Jack wouldn't let me": Will Friedwald, liner notes to Bing Crosby, *Bing: His Legendary Years, 1931 to 1957* (MCA/Decca, 1993).

96 "gold being poured out of a cup": Giddins, *Bing Crosby.*

97 "rhythm with romance": Friedwald, *Bing: His Legendary Years* liner notes.

98 In a 1953 essay: *Saturday Review,* June 27, 1953.

99 a pair of . . . parlor ballads: Giddins, *Bing Crosby,* pp. 375–76.

99 tripped over the Latin: Ibid., p. 379.

101 a record 375 prints: Patricia King Hanson and Carolyn B. Mitchell, eds., *The American Film Institute Catalog of Motion Pictures Produced in the United States: Feature Films, 1931–1940* (Los Angeles: University of California Press), p. 231.

102 The earliest transcription: Hugh Keyte and Andrew Parrot, eds., *The New Oxford Book of Carols* (New York: Oxford University Press, 1992), pp. 242–43.

102 the debut of "Silent Night": Ibid., pp. 304–5.

103 "the first break that I have ever had": Letter from IB to Jack Kapp, April 15, 1942, IBC-LC.

103 "I am not willing": Letter from IB to George Cohen, Jan. 14, 1941, IBC-LC.

104 "two boys and a girl setup . . . open only on holidays": *Holiday Inn* subject file, IBC-LC.

106 In one draft: Ibid.

108 Scharf remembered: Author interview with Walter Scharf.

108 "It was almost like a child": Ibid.

108 "nervous as a rabbit sniffing stew": *Los Angeles Mirror,* December 21, 1954.

108 "you won't have to worry": Ibid.

108 Crosby rolled his eyes: Author interview with Walter Scharf.

108 "He knew exactly": Ibid.

109 Scharf began by . . . "intuition it would be a special song": Ibid.

109 "a tremendously traumatic": Bergreen, *As Thousands Cheer,* p. 388.

110 "I'd never seen a man": Ibid.

110 "I'm sorry," Berlin said: Author interview with Walter Scharf.

111 "He just does anything": Letter from Fred Astaire to IB, July 1946, IBC-LC.

111 "I thought the first take": Charles Thompson, *Bing* (New York: David McKay, 1975), pp. 93–94.

112 home songs: For more on home songs see William W. Austin, *Susanna, Jeanie and The Old Folks at Home: The Songs of Stephen C. Foster from His Time to Ours* (New York: Macmillan, 1975); Nicholas Tawa, *Sweet Songs for Gentle Americans: The Parlor Song in America, 1790–1860* (New York: Popular Press, 1980); Nicholas Tawa, *A Music for the Millions: Antebellum Democratic Attitudes and the Birth of American Popular Music* (New York: Pendragon Press, 1984). Charles Hamm, *Yesterdays: Popular Song in America* (New York: W. W. Norton, 1979) also includes excellent discussions of several variations on the home song genre.

116 *Of all the Tin Pan Alley Greats:* Kimball and Emmet, *Complete Lyrics,* p. 492. For a trenchant discussion of Jews and blackface see Michael Rogin, *Blackface, White Noise: Jewish Immigrants in the Hollywood Melting Pot* (Los Angeles: University of California Press, 1996). Also see Melnick, *Right to Sing.*

118 Berlin refused invitations: Berlin, quoted in an unidentified newspaper clipping found in the songwriter's correspondence, IBC-LC: "The cast all lived together—in the Pacific and in Italy. There was no segregation, and we accepted no social engagements where all were not invited."

118 "outrageous" sentimental dream: See Leslie Fielder, "Come Back to the Raft Ag'in, Huck Honey," in *The New Fielder Reader* (New York: Prometheus Books, 1999).

119 He wrote in 1928: From the song "Let Me Sing and I'm Happy."

120 a fatal flub: The unreleased first take of "White Christmas" is included on Bing Crosby, *The Voice of Christmas: The Complete Decca Christmas Songbook* (MCA/Decca, 1998).

120 In an April letter: Letter from IB to Jack Kapp, April 15, 1942, IBC-LC.

121 "A jackdaw": Quotation found in "White Christmas" subject file, IBC-LC.

121 "However seasonal the words": Barrett, *Daughter's Memoir,* p. 209.

125 *What have we learned?*: *Chicago Times,* December 6, 1942.

125 *My new furnishings:* Vonnegut, *Mother Night,* p. 146.

127 an interventionist anthem: This didn't stop those on the opposite side of the issue from appropriating the song. On June 19, 1941, in the wake of the successful passage of the Lend-Lease Act pledging American support to the Allies, Martin Sweeney, a stridently anti-British isolationist member of the House of Representatives from Cleveland, Ohio, read into the Congressional Record a protest verse he'd composed to the tune of "God Bless America":

> *God save America from British rule:*
> *Stand beside her and guide her*
> *From the schemers who would make her a fool.*
> *From Lexington to Yorktown*
> *From blood-stained Valley Forge,*
> *God save America*
> *From a king named George.*

127 "Incidentally, every picture": *New York Times,* February 2, 1941.

129 "Songs make history": *New York Times,* May 17, 1942.

129 "I am delighted": Barrett, *Daughter's Memoir,* p. 195.

131 "14 songs by Irving Berlin": Quotation found in *Holiday Inn* subject file, IBC-LC.

131 "We know you haven't had much time": Ibid.

132 "At his present pace": Ibid.

133 Berlin was able to wire: Cable from IB to Mark Sandrich, August 5, 1942.

133 The *Times* referred: *New York Times,* August 5, 1942; *New York Herald-Tribune,* August 5, 1942; *Variety,* June 17, 1942.

133 murmurings . . . in the Berlin camp: Bergreen, *As Thousands Cheer,* p. 407.

133 "the greatest exploitation campaign": Letter from Dave Dreyer to IB, May 11, 1942, IBC-LC.

134 "Izzy is uptown": Bergreen, *As Thousands Cheer,* p. 73.

134 "I am as much of a song-plugger": Note from IB to Abel Green, 1954.

134 "You can't high-pressure": Letter from IB to George Cohen, November 6, 1940.

135 *Billboard* reported: *Billboard,* September 19, 1942.

135 the biggest the London office had ever handled: Cable from Louis Dreyfus to IB, September 15, 1942, IBC-LC.

135 "'Christmas' is our number one song": Cable from IB to Mark Sandrich, September 14, 1942, IBC-LC.

135 a "sensation": Cable from IB to Louis Dreyfus, September 15, 1942, IBC-LC.

135 a letter from Emanuel Sacks: Letter from Emanuel Sacks to IB, October 7, 1942, IBC-LC.

136 "one of the most phenomenal hits": *Billboard,* October 17, 1942.

136 "Irving Berlin is pretty upset": Undated clipping in Berlin scrapbooks, IBC-LC.

136 "Neither calendar makers": *Billboard,* October 31, 1942.

137 a boastful letter: Letter from IB to Mark Sandrich, November 2, 1942, IBC-LC.

137 A political cartoon: *New York Post,* November 27, 1942.

137 *Time* magazine proclaimed: *Time,* November 23, 1942.

137 "For the first time in many a year": *Jewish Times,* January 1, 1943.

137 An editorial: *Christian Science Monitor,* November 26, 1942.

138 According to one estimate: G. P. Mohrmann and F. Eugene Scott, "Popular Music and World War II: The Rhetoric of Continuation" in *Quarterly Journal of Speech,* Vol. 62, April 1976, p. 149.

139 "What this country needs": Perrett, *Days of Sadness,* p. 242.

139 William B. Lewis: Mohrmann and Scott, "Popular Music," p. 149.

139 "Songwriters ought to put their muses": *New York Herald-Tribune,* November 17, 1942.

139 Music War Committee: Mohrmann and Scott, "Popular Music," p. 147.

141 An estimated 75 percent: Millard, *America on Record,* p. 186.

142 "a new verse": Letter from IB to Saul Bornstein, May 14, 1942, IBC-LC.

142 "new words would not come": *American Weekly,* December 19, 1954.

143 *Men are longing: New York Herald-Tribune,* December 2, 1942. The poem was written by Jean Elliot.

143 "When Irving Berlin set 120,000,000": *Buffalo Courier-Express,* December 26, 1942.

144 Eddie Rickenbacker: *I'll Be Home for Christmas: The Library of Congress Revisits the Spirit of Christmas During World War II* (New York: Stonesong Press, 1999), pp. 41–43.

146 "I want you to cut the verse": Wilk, *They're Playing,* p. 276.

146 "We observed with considerable pleasure": *Detroit Free Press,* December 30, 1942.

147 "The boys in the South Pacific": *Boston American,* October 5, 1954.

147 A few prominent rabbis: Penne Restad, *Christmas in America* (New York: Oxford University Press, 1995), p. 158.

148 "It is significant": *I'll Be Home for Christmas,* p. 38.

148 *It wasn't just snow:* transcript of radio broadcast found in IBC-LC.

149 But polls taken: John W. Jeffries, *Wartime America: The World War II Home Front* (Chicago: Ivan R. Dee, 1996), pp. 171–72.

150 "So many young people": Thompson, *Bing*, p. 95.

150 Once, Crosby was entertaining: Quotation found in "White Christmas" subject file, IBC-LC.

150 Lyell Thompson, a squad leader: Letter from Lyell Thompsom to the author.

151 During Christmas, 1942: The following account was found in a letter to Berlin in the songwriter's papers, IBC-LC.

152 On Christmas Eve, 1944: *American Weekly*, December 19, 1954.

154 a double-CD compilation: on Bing Crosby, *The Voice of Christmas: The Complete Decca Christmas Songbook* (MCA/Decca, 1998).

157 The radio was playing: Roth, *Operation Shylock*, pp. 157–58.

158 "Kringle Jingles Ring the Bell": *Billboard*, December 23, 1943.

160 "a Christmas more uniform and secular": Restad, *Christmas in America*, p. 155.

162 When America Online: AOL computer poll, internet.

163 raucous carnival holiday: See Stephen Nissenbaum, *The Battle for Christmas* (New York: Random House, 1996). Other important sources on Christmas include Restad, *Christmas in America;* Karala Ann Marling, *Merry Christmas! Celebrating America's Greatest Holiday* (Cambridge: Harvard University Press, 2000); and William B. Waits, *The Modern Christmas in America* (New York: NYU Press, 1993).

164 Neil Gabler has observed: Neal Gabler, *An Empire of Their Own: How the Jews Invented Hollywood* (New York: Anchor Books, 1988), p. 4.

164 Philip Roth's outrageous: Roth, *Operation Shylock*, pp. 157–58.

169 "I do hope I'll see you": Letter from Fred Astaire to IB, December 18, 1970, IBC-LC.

169 *Another birthday:* Kimball and Emmet, *Complete Lyrics*, pp. 499–500.

174 it was a musical sea change: See Hamm, *Yesterdays*, pp. 338–39.

176 the emergence of Elvis Presley: Ibid., p. 404.

177 "Rock 'n' roll smells phony": Quoted on internet site: http://www.enteract.com/~salpap/rocknroll.htm

178 a popular disc jockey . . . In Portland, Oregon, radio station KEX: *Billboard,* December 16, 1957.

179 "Do you like the songs, Irving?": Furia, *Life in Song,* p. 251.

180 "I looked at myself": Ibid., pp. 256–57.

180 New York critics savaged the show: Bergreen, *As Thousands Cheer,* pp. 545–46.

183 "It was as if I owned a store": Kimball and Emmet, *Complete Lyrics,* p. xix.

184 "Seventy-one": Ibid., p. 498.

184 "As long as I'm able": Michael Freedland, *Irving Berlin* (New York: Stein and Day, 1974), p. 214.

184 "hunt-and-peck": Amy Asch, conversation with author.

185 *Old songs*: Kimball and Emmet, *Complete Lyrics,* p. 500.

188 "Ours has been": Cable from IB to Bing Crosby, December 3, 1953, IBC-LC.

188 "I see the picture 'White Christmas' ": Letter from Bing Crosby to IB, December 22, 1964, IBC-LC.

188 "I painted this about two years ago": Letter from IB to Bing Crosby, November 26, 1965, IBC-LC.

189 "It's a little late": Letter from IB to Bing Crosby, December 21, 1967, IBC-LC.

189 "I never cease to reflect": Letter from Bing Crosby to IB, December 26, 1967, IBC-LC.

190 "DEAR BING": Undated cable from IB to Bing Crosby, IBC-LC.

Index

Page numbers in *italics* refer to illustrations.

Permissions Acknowledgments